Managing Editor
Mara Ellen Guckian

Illustrator
Kelly McMahon

Editor in Chief
Ina Massler Levin, M.A.

Creative Director
Karen J. Goldfluss, M.S. Ed.

Cover Artist
Barb Lorseyedi

Art Coordinator
Renée Mc Elwee

Imaging
Craig Gunnell

Publisher

Mary D. Smith, M.S. Ed.

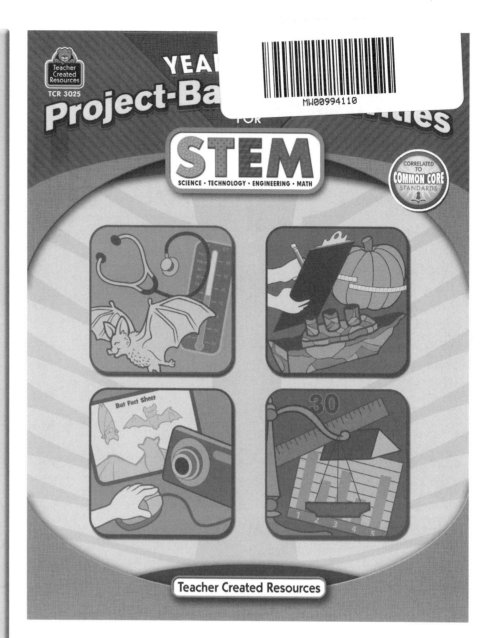

TCR 3025

YEAR
Project-Ba...   ...ities
FOR

STEM
SCIENCE · TECHNOLOGY · ENGINEERING · MATH

CORRELATED TO COMMON CORE STANDARDS

Bat Fact Sheet

30

Teacher Created Resources

Author
Stephanie Lester

Teacher Created Resources
12621 Western Avenue
Garden Grove, CA 92841
www.teachercreated.com
ISBN: 978-1-4206-3025-1

©2013 Teacher Created Resources
Reprinted, 2017
Made in U.S.A.

Teacher Created Resources

Table of Contents

Teacher Overview

Project-Based Units for STEM

Introduction

As educators, we are being required to place more emphasis on science, technology, engineering, and math (STEM) to insure that today's students will be prepared for the careers of tomorrow. Additionally, practicing important 21st century skills including collaboration, critical thinking, problem solving, and digital literacy should be part of our daily curricula. It is imperative AND a tall order. *Year Round Project-Based Activities for STEM* provides students with needed practice in these areas.

Project-based learning, simply put, is *learning by doing*. Project-based learning, or PBL, tends to be deeper learning that is more relevant to students and thus remembered longer. We need to educate students to be global competitors, and to do so we must require them to think creatively, to take risks, and to put what they are learning into practice. After all, it doesn't do much good to know a formula if you cannot put it to use.

In STEM curriculum, project-based learning is a must! Its collaborative style guarantees that 21st century skills are incorporated into the curriculum while supporting students' academic and socio-emotional growth. Further, PBL allows teachers to assess what students comprehend immediately, and adapt curriculum accordingly.

Standards, Benchmarks, and Learning Objectives

Each lesson in *Year Round Project-Based Activities for STEM (Grades 1–2)* meets one or more of the following standards for Science, Technology, and Mathematics, which are used with permission from McREL (Copyright 2012 McREL, Mid-continent Research for Education and Learning. Telephone 303-337-0990. Website: *www.mcrel.org.*). To align McREL Standards to the Common Core Standards go to www.mcrel.org. Additionally, age-appropriate learning objectives have been suggested for Engineering.

Science

Understands the structure and function of cells and organisms
➡ Knows the basic needs of plants and animals (e.g., air, water, nutrients, light or food, shelter)
➡ Knows that plants and animals have features that help them live in different environments

Understands the relationships among organisms and their physical environment
➡ Knows that plants and animals need certain resources for energy and growth (e.g., food, water, light, air)
➡ Knows that living things are found almost everywhere in the world and that distinct environments support the life of different types of plants and animals

Understands the structure and properties of matter
➡ Knows that different objects are made up of many different types of materials (e.g., cloth, paper, wood, metal) and have many different observable properties (e.g., color, size, shape, weight)
➡ Knows that things can be done to materials to change some of their properties (e.g., mixing, cutting, dissolving, bending, heating) but not all materials respond the same way to what is done to them

Understands the sources and properties of energy
➡ Knows that electricity in circuits can produce light, heat, sound, and magnetic effects

Understands forces and motion
➡ Knows that the position and motion of an object can be changed by pushing or pulling

Understands the nature of scientific knowledge
➡ Knows that scientific investigations generally work the same way in different places and normally produce results that can be duplicated.
➡ Understands that a model of something is different from the real thing (e.g., object, event)

Understands the nature of scientific inquiry
➡ Knows that learning can come from careful observations and simple experiments
➡ Knows that tools (e.g., magnifiers, rulers, balances, stethoscopes, timers) can be used to gather information
➡ Makes predictions based on patterns

Understands scientific enterprise
➡ Knows that in science it is helpful to work with a team and share findings with others

Standards, Benchmarks, and Learning Objectives *(cont.)*

Technology

Knows the characteristics and uses of computer hardware and operating systems

➡ Knows basic computer hardware (e.g., keyboard and mouse, printer and monitor, optical storage device (such as CD-ROM), case for the CPU [central processing unit])

➡ Powers-up computer and monitor, and starts a computer program
(e.g., checks that printer is switched on and online; reboots the computer when necessary)

➡ Knows the alphanumeric keys and special keys (e.g., function keys, escape key, space bar, delete/backspace, return/enter)

Knows the characteristics and uses of computer software programs

➡ Knows basic features of computer software (e.g., file, open, save, help, preview)

➡ Uses basic menu commands and toolbar functions

Understands the relationships among science, technology, society, and the individual

➡ Knows ways that technology is used at home and at school
(e.g., computers, cell phones, DVD players)

➡ Knows that new tools and ways of doing things affect all aspects of life, and may have positive or negative effects on other people

➡ Knows safe and responsible online behavior

Understands the nature of technological design

➡ Knows that both objects and systems occur in nature (e.g., stars and the solar system) but people can also design and make objects and systems (e.g., telephones and communication systems) to solve a problem and to improve the quality of life

➡ Knows that tools have specific functions, such as to observe, measure, create things, and do things more efficiently or easily; selecting the right tool makes the task easier

➡ Knows that people are always inventing new ways to solve problems and accomplish work (e.g., a computer is a machine that helps people work and play)

➡ Knows that planning is an important part of the design process

➡ Knows that new objects can be created out of physical materials (e.g., paper, cloth)

➡ Knows that because there may be multiple solutions to a design problem, each appropriate to different situations, many creative ideas can be useful

Understands the nature and uses of different forms of technology

➡ Knows that energy comes from different sources (e.g., electricity, gas, water) and is used in many common objects (e.g., a stove, some toys)

➡ Knows that there are different types of structures (e.g., house, airport, highway) and each one requires different materials and parts

Standards, Benchmarks, and Learning Objectives *(cont.)*

Engineering

Uses engineering design to pose questions, seek answers and develop solutions

➡ Identifies simple problems and solutions

➡ Understands troubleshooting procedures

➡ Proposes alternative solutions for procedures

➡ Uses tools, materials, and equipment associated with the building trades

➡ Understands elements of planning construction projects

➡ Uses a variety of verbal and graphic techniques to present conclusions

Mathematics

Uses a variety of strategies in the problem-solving process

➡ Uses discussions with others to understand problems

➡ Makes organized lists or tables of information necessary for solving a problem

Understands and applies basic and advanced properties of the concepts of numbers

➡ Counts whole numbers (i.e., both cardinal and ordinal numbers)

➡ Understands symbolic, concrete, and pictorial representations of numbers

Use basic and advanced procedures while performing the processes of computation

➡ Adds and subtracts whole numbers

➡ Solves real-world problems involving addition and subtraction of whole numbers

➡ Understands basic estimation strategies

Understands and applies basic and advanced properties of the concepts of measurement

➡ Understands the basic measurements of length, width, height, weight, and temperature

➡ Understands the concept of time and how it is measured

➡ Makes quantitative estimates of familiar linear dimensions, weights, and time intervals and checks them against measurements

Understands and applies basic and advanced properties of the concepts of geometry

➡ Understands basic properties of simple geometric shapes and similarities and differences between simple geometric shapes

➡ Understands the common language of spatial sense

Understands and applies basic and advanced concepts of statistics and data analysis

➡ Collects and represents information about objects or events in simple graphs

➡ Understands that one can find out about a group of things by studying just a few of them

Understands and applies basic and advanced concepts of probability

➡ Understands that some events are more likely to happen than others

➡ Understands that some events can be predicted fairly well but others cannot because we do not always know everything that may affect an event

Why Project-Based Learning?

The classroom is the perfect place to introduce project-based learning, incorporating both traditional academic and 21st century skills. The discovery-based activities in *Year Round Project-Based Activities for STEM* provide students, teachers, and parents with the following:

Opportunities for critical thinking—open-ended questions or prompts that lead to higher-level thinking, risk-taking, and investigation (solving problems versus finding the one correct answer)

Development of organizational skills—self regulation, planning, and sequencing to use the information provided or researched (learning how to implement ideas and use all the information gathered)

Options for creativity—activities that allow for innovative strategies or solutions to be shared (a reminder that creativity is not for the select few—we can all be creative with practice)

Practice communicating—sharing ideas, theories, discoveries; using appropriate vocabulary; demonstrating understanding through drawings, graphs, charts, etc. (developing social skills necessary to work in groups)

Relevance—activities related to students' lives make the concepts being taught more meaningful, and thus more memorable (global awareness activities)

Time for collaboration—social learning in a classroom and via technology (helps students internalize their observations, initiate higher-level thinking, and see the bigger picture)

Uses for technology as a tool to develop digital literacy—performing tasks effectively in a digital environment by incorporating interactive whiteboards; Skype; webcams and web videos; videotaping; publishing to create props such as labels, signs, and charts

Use the discovery-based projects in this book to get a feel for what project-based learning is all about. Later you can develop your own PBL units with a deeper understanding of the process. Listen. What do your students *want* to learn about, and how can that interest be facilitated? The 21st century vocabulary listed on the following page is a collection of action words to help motivate and direct you and your students. What are you waiting for? It is time to get started!

21st Century Vocabulary

apply	critique	hypothesize	observe
arrange	design	imagine	organize
assess	determine	implement	plan
brainstorm	develop	improve	practice
challenge	discover	improvise	predict
chart	discuss	incorporate	problem-solve
clarify	document	initiate	question
collaborate	dramatize	innovate	record
communicate	estimate	inquire	relate
compare	evaluate	invent	research
complete	experiment	investigate	review
consider	explain	list	specify
construct	explore	listen	study
coordinate	gather	model	support
create	graph	modify	theorize

Websites to Assist PBL

The following sites were chosen to support each project-based unit in this book. Take time at the beginning of each unit to tour the sites and familiarize yourself with their offerings. Some provide pictures and others have short informative videos on unit topics. Many sites offer additional activity ideas, worksheets, and suggestions for games. It is up to you to determine if you will incorporate a site into your students' activities, use it for research, or for background information. All have something special to offer. By preparing ahead of time, you will know just where to go to enhance your students discoveries and help extend their explorations.

Bats

Bats Bats Everywhere—*www.bats4kids.org/*
Where bats live, what type of homes they occupy, and how they help humans. The big nine bat facts are discussed.

Defenders of Wildlife—*www.defenders.org/bats/basic-facts*
Information about the size, behavior, diet, habitat, life span, and appearance of the bat.

KidzCave—Bat Conservation International, Inc.—
http://www.batcon.org/index.php/all-about-bats/kidz-cave.html
The main site offers information about bats, and bat conservation. Additional age-appropriate materials and a video about echolocation can be found in the Kidz Cave.

KidZone Bats—*www.kidzone.ws/animals/bats/index.htm*
Support the bat unit with printable activity worksheets, online activities, facts, and photos.

Buoyancy

eHow—*www.ehow.com/how_8159938_teach-buoyancy-grade-school-children.html*
This site suggests several experiments to extend the concept of buoyancy.

Mythbusters Discovery—
http://dsc.discovery.com/videos/mythbusters-lets-talk-buoyancy.html
Watch the "Let's Talk Buoyancy" video and listen to the Mythbusters discuss the science behind why boats float.

Exploring Color

Activities for Kids—*http://activitiesforkids.com/printable-color-wheel*
Check out different color wheel activities and an idea for a magic potion drink to show color mixing—a "must try" beverage, and so simple!

First School—*www.first-school.ws/activities/artapp/rainbow-color-mixing.htm*
This site provides good illustrations of a rainbow and primary and secondary colors.

Websites to Assist PBL *(cont.)*

Pumpkins

All About Pumpkins—*http://www.allaboutpumpkins.com/*
This site offers all kinds of facts about pumpkins from the Jack Creek Farm including information about growing, storing, and cooking with pumpkins. This family-owned-and-run farm has been in the pumpkin business for generations.

Cool Pumpkin Facts—*http://www.kids-learn.org/pumpkins/coolfacts.htm*
First grade students go to the local pumpkin patch and find the parts of the pumpkin life cycle.

Pumpkin Facts for Kids—*http://www.ask.com/questions-about/Pumpkin-Facts-for-Kids*
Teachers needing answers will benefit from the information here and get ideas for pumpkin planting, cooking projects, and crafts. There is even a recipe for pumpkin pancakes!

Pumpkin Patch—*http://www.youtube.com/watch?v=6L1_48gel1Y&feature=related*
The basic pumpkin facts provided in this video are a great starting place for this unit.

The Pumpkin Patch—*http://www.pumpkin-patch.com/facts.html*
This site provides information about pumpkins, gourds, and Indian corn, as well as pictures and student activities—all from the 25 acres at Live Oak Canyon Farm in California.

Healthy Hearts

American Heart Association—*http://www.heart.org/HEARTORG/GettingHealthy/ HealthierKids/Healthier-Kids_UCM_304156_SubHomePage.jsp*
This American Heart Association resource is working to help kids and families live heart-healthy lives. This site provides resources regarding healthy living tips.

KidsHealth—*http://kidshealth.org/kid/htbw/heart.html*
This site gives facts about your heart and circulatory system.

Science Kids—*http://www.sciencekids.co.nz/sciencefacts/humanbody/heart.html*
Enjoy the fun heart facts for kids and learn some interesting new facts and information about how the amazing human heart works.

Women's and Children's Health Network—*http://www.cyh.com/HealthTopics/ HealthTopicDetailsKids.aspx?p=335&np=152&id=1446*
This site offers quick answers to simple questions. What does your heart look like? What does it do? How do you keep it healthy?

Websites to Assist PBL *(cont.)*

Spiders

Kidzone—*www.kidzone.ws/lw/spiders/index.htm*
This site, suitable for Kindergarten through Grade 6, offers fun facts for kids, spider photos, and printable activity worksheets.

Spiderzrule—*www.spiderzrule.com/*
Here you'll find a huge amount of information and pictures about spiders— from the deadliest funnel web spider to the harmless garden orb weaver. And don't miss the section of spider songs!

Spider Photo Gallery, Nature Photo—*http://www.naturephoto-cz.com/invertebrates.html*
View excellent photographs of all types of spiders in their habitats.

Static Electricity

Explain that Stuff—*http://www.explainthatstuff.com/electricity.html*
This site provides simple explanations for electricity and static electricity and offers examples—a quick way for a teacher to get up to speed!

Science Kids—Fun Science and technology for kids!—
http://www.sciencekids.co.nz/electricity.html
Check out the exciting subject of electricity for kids with an array of experiments, games, projects, quizzes, interesting facts, amazing videos, worksheets, and more!

Alliant Energy Kids— *http://www.alliantenergykids.com/EnergyBasics/index.htm*
Here's a site that is easy to navigate and provides fun facts, games and activities, and a teacher section, all about electricity.

Three-Dimensional Designs

Ben's Guide—*http://bensguide.gpo.gov/k-2/neighborhood/*
Click on the simple neighborhood map and learn more about the activities and occupations in a building such as a library or a police station.

Primary Resources—*http://www.primaryresources.co.uk/maths/mathsE3.htm*
This site from the UK offers activities and patterns for 2-D and 3-D shapes, including an interesting way to use interlocking pattern blocks.

Topic Box—*http://www.topicbox.net/mathematics/3d_shape/*
This site provides information and games about all kinds of math topics, including shapes. You can download nets (patterns) and show a presentation to illustrate 1-D, 2-D, and 3-D shapes.

Why Teach STEM Curricula?

Children are naturally curious and love to investigate. The STEM approach to teaching is inquiry-based, which is defined as the process of asking questions and trying to find answers for those questions. The components of STEM—*science, technology, engineering,* and *mathematics*, all combine to offer students a vast array of highly engaging learning experiences in which teachers are able to capitalize on students' strong desire to learn about the world around them. This resource is for the educator who recognizes that the true task for a teacher is to assist students in developing a deeper knowledge of STEM subjects combined with the 21st century skills they will need to be successful.

Utilizing the philosophy of STEM allows educators to capitalize on the natural tendencies of young learners. Young students are, by nature, scientists and engineers—willing and eager to experiment, discover new things, and build and take apart anything they can get their hands on. The best way to capture and build their interest and excitement is to introduce science and engineering at an early age.

STEM-based projects are highly engaging, fun, and full of natural learning opportunities. These experiences will broaden students' world views, encourage them to think critically, and provide ample opportunities to connect and apply concepts learned to their everyday experiences.

Every effort has been made to include experiments and activities in this resource that use everyday materials, are easy to understand and facilitate, and ignite a desire for further learning!

Remember, an enthusiastic teacher introducing a concept is much more effective in developing successful project-based learning activities than a teacher with an extensive knowledge background who does not understand how to build the connections that facilitate learning for young students. Teachers who utilize everyday experiences and the numerous opportunities for incidental learning throughout the day understand how to best maximize those learning connections and implement project-based learning for young children.

Using the STEM approach to teach effectively requires a combination of introducing engaging materials while balancing the fun with the purposeful integration of connective activities that encourage the development of high-level, critical-thinking skills. Students are more likely to retain the knowledge gained through this approach as well as develop confidence and self-direction as they learn to work both cooperatively and independently.

How to Teach STEM Curricula

The activities in this book will enable you to introduce your students to the wonderful world of project-based learning using the STEM approach!

The four content areas of STEM are an integral part of everyday life and are naturally engaging for young students. At every opportunity, offer the following approaches to learning.

Science

- Compare and contrast different attributes of items.

- Encourage student-directed exploration using magnifying glasses, microscopes, measuring tools, scales and balances, and other scientific instruments.

- Complete experiments utilizing the scientific method—*predict, observe, record,* and *evaluate.*

Technology

- Offer opportunities for students to research online using computers.

- Utilize microscopes, electronic devices, cameras, interactive white boards, etc.

- Investigate and present research using webcams, web videos, presentation slide shows, and interactive whiteboards.

Engineering

- Provide activities that require the students to solve a problem using the process of planning, designing, experimenting, making changes, and sharing.

    Plan: Create a solution that best solves the problem.

    Design: Find and/or create the necessary materials and plans needed to perform the experiment.

    Experiment: Perform the experiment, redesign, and experiment as necessary.

    Share: Evaluate the outcome, explain the design, and discuss why it did, or did not work. Include information regarding the process that was followed and the changes that were made in order to successfully solve the problem.

Math

- Encourage student-directed exploration using various measurement tools, including measuring tapes, scales, balances, yardsticks, meter sticks, and rulers.

- Provide opportunities for students to practice estimating and predicting.

- Introduce and reinforce mathematical concepts (number sense, shapes, number lines, counting, addition and subtraction, fractions, greater than and less than, etc.).

Set Up STEM Discovery Centers

Maximize your students' learning capabilities and further develop their higher-level thinking skills by providing year-round STEM discovery centers in addition to your music, writing, and art areas. The following are some of the skills students will develop while utilizing these centers:

- applying concepts introduced previously
- brainstorming
- critical thinking
- collaborating
- decision making

- experimenting
- predicting, observing, recording, documenting, and evaluating findings
- planning (start-to-finish task skills)
- researching (in books and online)

All established centers should have clipboards, different types and colors of paper, writing implements, tape and glue, staplers, scissors, and appropriate book selections. Time should be scheduled **daily** to allow students the freedom to explore at self-selected discovery centers. Music of different types would make a great accompaniment at this time.

Suggestions for materials to include in these ongoing STEM discovery centers are listed on page 15. Add or switch out items as interest grows and/or materials present themselves.

Once your classroom centers are arranged, share the parent letter (page 16) with parents, and prepare to immerse yourselves in discovery-based projects!

Start with one of the projects in this book that relates to your students' interests. All the information and instructions you'll need have been included for each unit, but do not limit the students to those ideas. Encourage input from students, especially during brainstorming sessions.

Initially, as the teacher, it may be necessary to reassure your students that every idea will be considered, and to provide directed times during which each student takes turns sharing an idea with the group. This will develop a foundation of acceptance and value for each member of the group that is essential to the success of project-based learning.

Consider potential outcomes from exploring the chosen unit. Images of what the discovery process should look like may begin to form in your mind. Don't become too attached to these ideas, though; your students should be the engineers. Encourage them to invent and create things as needed to solve the problems or questions presented. Remember, it is about the *process of learning, and not finding one "correct" answer.*

As your students complete these discovery-based projects, they will be developing the life skills necessary to become successful problem solvers.

STEM Discovery Center Tools

Science

clipboards
digital cameras
fish (living)
magnets
magnifying glasses

microscope
mirrors
nonfiction books
plants (living)
nature objects (rocks, shells, etc.)

Technology

calculators
computers
digital camera
interactive whiteboards
laptops/tablets

microscope
overhead projector
tape recorder/voice recorder
timers
video camera

Engineering

art materials
balances
blocks
boxes (all sizes)
building materials
cardboard
clipboards
construction materials
construction tools
containers

glue
office supplies
recycled materials
rulers and yardsticks
staplers
string
Styrofoam®
tape (all kinds)
Velcro®
wood

Mathematics

3-D shapes
balances
counters
counting bears
counting cubes
dice
dominoes
manipulatives
number lines
patterns and tracers

poker chips
rulers
scales
shape templates
solid shapes
tape measure
thermometer
wooden blocks
yard sticks/meter sticks

Date: _____

Dear Families,

This year we will be completing several project-based learning activities utilizing the STEM approach to learning. Children are naturally full of curiosity and love to investigate. The components of STEM – science, technology, engineering, and mathematics – all combine to offer students a vast array of highly engaging learning experiences in which teachers are able to capitalize on a student's strong desire to learn about the world around him or her.

It is very exciting to have this opportunity to assist your child in developing the skills that will be needed to find answers and solutions for problems unknown to us at this time. The STEM approach to teaching is inquiry-based, which is defined as the process of asking questions and trying to find answers for those questions. The following academic areas will be strengthened through STEM projects:

Science: Predicting, observing, recording, and evaluating

Technology: Utilizing computers and other technology to solve problems and find answers

Engineering: Designing a plan to solve a problem

Mathematics: Utilizing math concepts to calculate and solve problems

Families will be asked to collaborate with their children to complete family connection activities that will be sent home to reinforce different STEM activities. Please ask your child to explain the project-based learning activity that was completed that day in class. Return the completed family connection page for your child to share in class. Along with the family connections worksheets, we will also occasionally be requesting donations of specific items to use to complete our STEM projects.

We appreciate your support of our STEM projects throughout the year.

Sincerely,

_____

Bats, Bats, Bats

STEM Objectives

1. Students will conduct research about bats and share the information.

2. Students will create models of the bats they have researched and conduct an experiment to better understand the importance of bats to our environment.

3. Bat data will be collected, recorded, and evaluated using charts, graphs, and/or spreadsheets.

Introduce the Topic – Bats

1. Read a nonfiction book about bats. Then discuss the characteristics of bats to introduce appropriate vocabulary. (See page 19.)

2. Discuss the roles that bats play in our world.

3. Share nonfiction and fiction books about bats. Discuss each book after it has been read, and keep copies on display.

Suggestions

Bats by Gail Gibbons

Bats (Eye to Eye with Endangered Species) by Cindy Rodriquez

Bats (Usborne Beginners Nature) by Megan Cullis, Connie McLennan, and Sue King

National Geographic Readers: Bats by Elizabeth Carney

Scholastic Reader Level 1: Bats by Lily Wood and Linda C. Wood

Stellaluna by Janell Cannon

Time For Kids: Bats! by Editors of TIME For Kids

Understanding Bats by Kim Williams

Zipping, Zapping, Zooming Bats (Let's-Read-and-Find-Out Science 2) by Ann Earle

4. Provide opportunities for students to go online for additional information and to check the suggested bat websites on page 9.

Bats, Bats, Bats *(cont.)*

Brainstorming Sessions

1. Help students list what they already know about bats (fact and fiction). You may wish to create a web or another type of graphic organizer, such as a KWL chart.

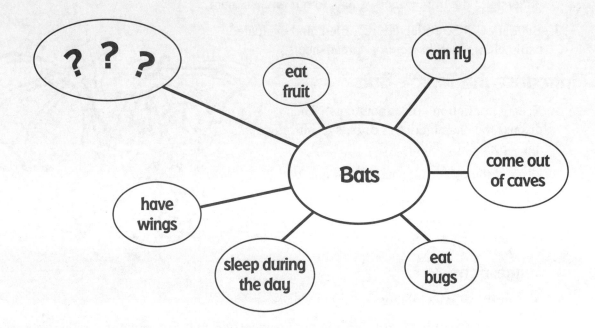

2. Create a list of questions to discuss related to bats. Start with these:

   • How many different types of bats are there?

   • Why are people afraid of bats?

   • What is the difference between microbats and megabats?

   • How do bats help our environment?

   • How can humans help to keep bats safe?

   • How can we help others to treat bats respectfully and appreciate how they help our environment?

Bat Vocabulary

A **bat** is a nocturnal, mouse-like, flying mammal. To fly, it uses wings formed by the membranes connecting its body to its forearms. Like most **mammals,** bats are warm-blooded vertebrates with hair. Females produce milk to nourish their young.

Some bats **hibernate** in cold weather in caves, mines, or hollow trees. Hibernating is like a deep sleep. Hibernation protects animals from the cold when food is scarce.

Bats, like dolphins, use **echolocation** to navigate. They make high-pitched sounds and listen for the echoes to determine the direction and distance of objects in their paths.

There are many kinds of bats. The most common bats are known as **microbats,** and they can be found all over the world. Many eat insects. Others, called **megabats**, or fruit bats, are larger Old World bats. They tend to eat fruit and live only in warmer tropical regions of the world.

Some species of Old and New World bats have a **nose leaf**, which is a thin, broad, membranous fold of skin. It varies greatly in size and form from one species of bat to another.

Bats, Bats, Bats

The following project-based bat activities are designed to encourage collaborative learning and discovery. Students should work in small groups (4 to 6). Encourage students to notice when they are using *science*, *technology*, *engineering*, or *math* during their bat explorations.

Supplies

- 200 small manipulatives (counters, cubes, counting chips, etc.)
- small paper or plastic bag (one per student)
- timer or stopwatch to time 30-second increments
- whistle or bell
- modeling dough ("bat dough" recipe on page 21), ½ cup per student
- ½ cup measuring cups
- bases for sculptures—cardboard or heavy paper plates (one per student)
- plastic knives and shaping tools
- fine-tipped markers, permanent markers
- tempera paint—black, brown, white, and other bat colors
- paintbrushes—variety of sizes
- crayons, colored pencils, pencils
- *Bats to the Rescue* recording sheet (page 25)
- *Bat Fact Sheet* (page 26)
- hand washing area, soap, water, and towels
- nonfiction and fiction books about bats (See page 17 for suggestions.)
- bat research websites (See page 9 for suggestions.)

Teacher Preparation

1. Consider making the modeling dough (or at least the kneading part) as another activity prior to starting this project. Display a copy of the recipe card.

2. Print copies of the *Bats to the Rescue* recording sheet and the *Bat Fact Sheet* for each student.

3. Identify a large, open area where the initial activity will take place. It will need to be large enough to spread out the 200 manipulatives and have room for all the students to move around.

4. Familiarize yourself with the characteristics of bats to guide the student discussions.

5. Set up approved bat research websites for students to view.

6. Create a sign-up sheet or checklist to insure that a variety of different bats are chosen to be sculpted. Create additional charts, graphs, or spreadsheets as needed to record group responses.

7. Arrange the materials, recording sheets, and writing implements near prepared student work areas and stations.

Bat Sculptures

Name of Bat	Sculptor
Brown Bat	Jennie
Flying Fox	Colton
Fruit Bat	Carri

Bats, Bats, Bats *(cont.)*

Student Preparation

1. Review the characteristics of bats and the questions from the brainstorming session. Has any new information been discovered that can be added to the web or KWL chart?

2. Review the bat vocabulary on page 19. Post a laminated copy of the page in the research area.

3. Discuss and chart any additional bat facts discovered.

Introduce the *Bats, Bats, Bats* Activities

1. Explain that students will be doing an activity to see just how helpful bats can be, and how necessary they are to our ecosystems. Information from the activity will be recorded on a *Bats to the Rescue* recording sheet.

2. Outline the process of choosing a type of bat for a sculpture and how to research to discover three facts about the bat.

3. Distribute a fact sheet to each student. Model how to record the facts on the *Bat Fact Sheet* page.

4. Review the classroom rules for working with dough. Explain that one of their activities will involve making dough models of the bats chosen to research, and that their *Bat Fact Sheets* will be displayed with the finished bat sculptures.

5. Encourage students to use the new vocabulary words when completing the activities.

Bat Dough

Ingredients

- 2 cups of flour (plus 1/4 cup for kneading)
- 1 cup salt
- 2 cups boiling water
- 1 tablespoon vegetable oil
- 1 teaspoon cream of tartar

Procedure

1. Mix all ingredients together.
2. Cook on HIGH in a microwave for 1 minute.
3. Stir the mixture and return it to the microwave for approximately 1 more minute.
4. Leave to cool.
5. Knead on a floured board. Add more flour if dough is sticky.

Bats, Bats, Bats *(cont.)*

"Bats to the Rescue" Game *– Science/ Engineering/Math*

Tools

- 200 small manipulatives (counters, cubes, counting chips, etc.)
- small paper or plastic bag (one per student)
- timer or stopwatch to time 30-second increments
- whistle or bell (optional)
- *Bats to the Rescue* recording sheets
- writing implements

Procedure (whole group)

Round 1

1. Have students spread out the 200 manipulatives in a large, open area. Explain that the manipulatives represent mosquitos and students will be bats.
2. Each student "bat" will use a bag to collect (eat) as many mosquitoes as he or she can in 30 seconds once the signal to start (Go!) has been given and the timer has been started.
3. At the 30-second signal (Stop!), the student bats will stop collecting food.
4. Students will count the insects remaining in the area, **not** the ones in their bags.
5. Record the number of mosquitoes not collected on the *Bats to the Rescue* recording sheet.

Round 2

1. Announce that half the bats got trapped in buildings and died. These bats will not be out hunting insects for the second round.
2. Identify which half of the students will not go out hunting for the second round.
3. Repeat steps 1–5 from Round 1. This time only **half** the students will be bats.

Round 3

1. Announce that half of the remaining bats were disturbed during their hibernation and didn't make it through the winter.
2. Identify which half of the remaining students will not go out hunting for the third round.
3. Repeat steps 1–5 from Round 1. This time **one-quarter** of the students will be bats.

Culmination

1. Review the data on the *Bats to the Rescue* recording sheet.
2. Evaluate the impact of bats dying and the effect on our mosquito population.

Bats, Bats, Bats *(cont.)*

Station 1 – Research a Bat – *Science/Technology/Engineering/Math*

Tools

- nonfiction books and posters about bats
- pencils, colored pencils, fine-tipped markers, crayons
- *Bat Fact Sheet*
- computer /Internet access

Procedure

1. Look through several books about bats or online on approved sites.

2. Choose one bat to focus on.

3. Identify three facts about the bat chosen. Look for information that will help create your bat or that viewers might find interesting.

4. Record the bat name and the three bat facts on your *Bat Fact Sheet*.

5. Add a detailed drawing of the bat to the page.

Station 2 – Make a Bat Sculpture – *Science/Technology/Engineering/Math*

Tools

- bases for sculptures—cardboard or heavy paper plates (one per student)
- tempera paint—black, brown, white, and other bat colors
- modeling dough (½ cup per student)
- ½ cup measuring cups
- paintbrushes—variety of sizes
- permanent markers
- plastic knives and shaping tools
- completed *Bat Fact Sheet*

Procedure

1. Measure out ½ cup of dough and arrange the dough on the base.
2. Use your drawing and other available pictures as guides to form the bat.
3. Pay attention to the head shape, ears, and wing formation.
4. Add details as desired to the bat and to the base.
5. When the sculpture is dry, paint it and display the *Bat Fact Sheet* near it.

Bats, Bats, Bats *(cont.)*

Culminating STEM Activities

1. Display the bats in two groups, Megabats and Microbats. Students may need to do additional research to determine which group their bats belong to.

2. Ask each student to stand by his or her model and share the three facts about his or her bat. Consider filming presentations to share with parents.

3. Plan a "Bat Museum Day." Invite another classroom to view your bat research projects. Invite family members to come in and view the students' bat models and facts.

4. Send home the Family Connection letter (page 27) to complete collaboratively. When the pages are returned, create or add to a list titled "Bats are Beneficial."

5. Invite a member of a local bat organization to come and speak to your class.

6. Play a bat echolocation game in an open area, preferably a grassy one outside. One child, who is comfortable being blindfolded, will "get to be" the bat. The other children will be the insects and other foods the bat will find.

Beep, Beep, Buzz, Buzz Game

1. To play, have the blindfolded "bat" in the center of the group of "insects."

2. Explain to the blindfolded child that, like a bat using echolocation to find its food and avoid obstacles, he or she will listen closely and try to catch dinner.

   The bat will make beeping sounds. ***Beep, Beep, Beep…***

3. The insects, in turn, will make buzzing sounds. ***Buzz, Buzz, Buzz…***

4. Bat and insects continue to make sounds while moving around.

5. When a bat catches (tags) an insect, the insect can take the place of the bat, or go to a bat cave area while the game continues.

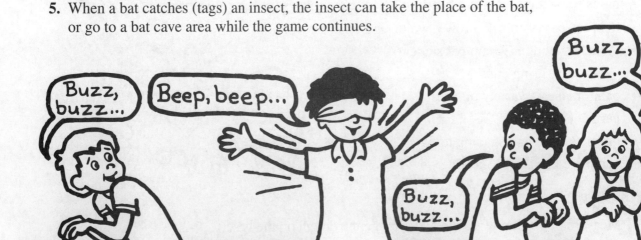

Name:

Bats to the Rescue

Round #	Number of Bats	Number of Mosquitos Left
1		
2		
3		

Observation

When there are less bats there are _____ mosquitoes.

Why do you think bats are helpful? _____

_____

_____

Name:

Bats to the Rescue

Round #	Number of Bats	Number of Mosquitos Left
1		
2		
3		

Observation

When there are less bats there are _____ mosquitoes.

Why do you think bats are helpful? _____

_____

_____

Bat Fact Sheet

My bat is called _____ .

Here are three facts about this bat:

1. _____

2. _____

3. _____

This is _____ bat.

Student's Name _____

Date:_____

Hello,

We are completing a project-based STEM project about **BATS**! Your child has completed several activities and is discovering many facts about bats. Ask your child to tell you some of the surprising facts that we have discovered about bats. Did you know. . .

1. Bats are very helpful animals and have important roles in nature.

2. Microbats eat insects and keep the mosquito population under control.

3. Some species of bats, such as the Little Brown Bat, can eat 500–1,000 mosquitoes in one hour. That can add up to eating 4,000–8,000 mosquitos in an 8-hour night!

4. Megabats eat fruit and then spread fruit seeds throughout the forest. This is an important means of ensuring new plants grow in the forests.

5. Most microbats are very small (the size of a house mouse) and most megabats are larger (the size of a squirrel).

Directions

1. Discuss the role of bats in our world with your child. Can you think of additional benefits?

2. Have your child choose one of the benefits to humans to write about and illustrate below.

Bats help our world by . . .

_____

_____

Buoyancy and Boat Design

STEM Objectives

1. Students will research, investigate, and experiment to find out how a boat's design affects its buoyancy.

2. Students will create boats to determine which design will support the most weight without sinking.

3. Students will be able to explain why some boat designs work better than others.

4. Data will be collected, recorded, and evaluated using charts, graphs, and/or spreadsheets.

Introduce the Topic – Buoyancy

1. Read a nonfiction book about buoyancy. Then discuss the concepts of buoyancy using appropriate vocabulary. (See page 30.)

2. Share nonfiction and fiction books about water vessels and buoyancy. Discuss each book after it has been read and keep copies on display.

Suggestions

Early Reader: Sink or Float? by Lynn Salem and Josie Stewart

Floating and Sinking (First Facts: Our Physical World) by Ellen Sturm Niz

Red Fox and His Canoe (I Can Read Book 1) by Nathaniel Benchley and Arnold Lobel

What Floats? What Sinks?: A Look at Density by Jennifer Boothroyd

Will It Float or Sink? (Rookie Read-About Science) by Melissa Stewart

3. Talk about sinking and floating. Experiment with some classroom objects and a container filled with water. Before each item is placed in the water, vote on whether it will sink or float. Add the term "buoyant" when discussing the items that float to help students make connections.

4. Provide opportunities for students to go online for additional information and check the suggested buoyancy websites on page 9.

Buoyancy and Boat Design *(cont.)*

Brainstorming Sessions

1. Help students list what they already know about *buoyancy* on a KWL chart.

2. Create a list of questions to discuss related to buoyancy. Start with these:

- Can heavy objects float?
- What happens if you put a heavy object on something like a raft?
- Are you buoyant? (Yes, you can float if you lay flat. Your body has air in it. A penny cannot float by itself, even though it is little, because there is no air in it.)
- Why are there different designs for boats?
- What type of boat designs carry heavy loads?
- What type of boat designs would go fast?
- What boat designs might hold the most weight without sinking?

Buoyancy		
K	**W**	**L**
Some things don't sink. Ducks don't sink on the water. Boats can float.		

Buoyancy and Boat Design Vocabulary

buoyancy—an object's ability to float in water (or air, or other liquid); the power of a liquid to keep something afloat

hull—the main body of a ship or large boat including the bottom, sides, and deck

surface area—the part of an object that is exposed to the surface of the water

water displacement—the water that is pushed away by an object

vessel—ship or large boat; a hollow container

Explanations

1. When an object is placed in the water, it pushes water out of the way.

   - If the object weighs less than the amount of water that is pushed out of the way, the object will **float**.

   - If the object weighs more than the amount of water that is pushed out of the way, the object will **sink**.

2. Increasing the surface area of a boat increases the amount of water that it pushes away without increasing the weight of the boat, and that allows a larger boat to float.

Float   **Sink**

Buoyancy and Boat Design

The following project-based buoyancy activities are designed to encourage collaborative learning and discovery. Students can work independently or in small groups (3 to 4) depending on the setup for each activity. Encourage students to notice when they are using *science, technology, engineering*, or *math* during their buoyancy explorations.

Supplies

- one or more large containers of water (Clear storage bins can accommodate 2–3 students.)
- nonfiction and fiction books about buoyancy (See page 28 for suggestions.)
- aluminum foil (two 4" x 6" pieces for each student)
- butcher paper (for large graph)
- examples of different types of boats
- pictures of different types of boats
- scale *(optional)*
- fan *(optional)*
- *Boat Designs* recording sheet (page 36)
- pencils, crayons, fine-tipped markers, permanent markers
- buoyancy research websites (See page 9 for suggestions)
- pennies or other uniform-sized counters (30–50 per student at a water station.)

Teacher Preparation

1. Print a *Boat Designs* recording sheet for each student.

2. Familiarize yourself with the vocabulary (See page 30.), concepts of buoyancy, and different types of boat designs.

3. Display examples and pictures of several types of boats for the students to refer to during the activities. Ask students to name as many different types of boats as they can and compare them. Does it carry people or products? Is it for work or pleasure? How much could it carry? End the discussion by focusing on the bottom shape of each boat. Does the boat have a flat or a V-shaped hull?

   - airboat
   - barge
   - canoe
   - catamaran

   - fishing boat
   - kayak
   - rowboat
   - sailboat

   - container ship
   - cruise ship
   - dingy
   - ferry

   - speed boat
   - tanker
   - tugboat
   - yacht

4. Create a graph so that each student can record the number of objects that his/her boat held before sinking. (See Station 3 on page 34.)

5. Create additional charts, graphs, or spreadsheets as needed to record group responses and as part of the culminating events.

6. Arrange stations where students can research and design boats, construct boats, then complete their buoyancy experiments.

Buoyancy and Boat Design *(cont.)*

Student Preparation

1. Review the concept of buoyancy and other information from the brainstorming sessions. Ask if any new information has been discovered which can be added to the KWL chart.

2. If appropriate, set up a **Sink** or **Float** station in the classroom and allow students time to test different items before beginning the *Buoyancy and Boat Design* activities.

3. Ask students to name as many types of boats as they can. Discuss the examples of boats and the purpose of different boat designs.

4. Post an enlarged copy of the vocabulary page and/or ask students to create illustrated vocabulary word cards.

Introduce *Buoyancy and Boat Design* Activities

1. Divide the students into small groups to complete their buoyancy activities. Determine how many students can be in each station at a time.

2. Explain that each student will be designing and creating two boats using aluminum foil and then conducting experiments to determine how many pennies each boat can hold without sinking.

3. Outline the process of designing the boats using aluminum foil. Explain how to research to find ideas for different hull designs.

4. Establish Station 1 in the reading area, or create the research station at a table near the computer.

5. Model how to create a plan for the boats on the *Boat Designs* recording sheet. (See page 36.) Each student will create two different hull designs (narrow, wide, thick, or thin).

6. Distribute a *Boat Designs* recording sheet to each student. Encourage students to refer back to their resources as needed and to use the new vocabulary words when completing the activities.

7. Explain how to proceed at each work area. Model how to use the materials, if necessary, and remind student-engineers that they are designing and creating a boat for a specific purpose— to hold the most weight (mass).

Buoyancy and Boat Design *(cont.)*

Station 1 – Research and Design Boats – *Science/Technology/Engineering/Math*

Tools

- nonfiction books, posters, and pictures about boats and water vessels
- examples of different types of boats
- access to approved *buoyancy* and *boat* websites
- pencils, colored pencils, fine-tipped markers, crayons
- *Boat Designs* recording sheet *(for each student)*

Procedure

1. Look through several books about boats and compare examples. Research boats online and print out pictures.

2. Choose two different boat designs and draw them on your *Boat Designs* recording sheet. One boat should have a narrow bottom and one boat should have a wider, flat bottom.

3. Add details to your boat designs on your planning sheet.

4. Label each boat design—*narrow, wide, round, square, rectangular, oval,* or other words.

Station 2 – Constructing Boats – *Science/Engineering/Math*

Tools

- aluminum foil (two 4" x 6" pieces for each student)
- scissors
- pencils, crayons, fine-tipped markers, permanent markers (to add details to boats)
- *Boat Designs* recording sheet
- nonfiction and fiction books about buoyancy

Procedure

1. Construct your boats following the designs that you drew. Use your drawings, pictures, websites, and books as guides.

2. Bend or fold the foil to create the hulls of each boat. Trim it with scissors if needed.

3. Label your boats **Boat 1** and **Boat 2**. Add your initials.

4. Add extra details to your boats with the permanent markers, if desired.

Buoyancy and Boat Design *(cont.)*

Station 3 – Prediction and Experimentation *– Science/Engineering/Math*

Tools

- 2 boats per student, labeled **Boat 1** and **Boat 2**
- large tubs of water (clear storage bins work well)
- *Boat Designs* recording sheet and pencils
- butcher paper for class graph
- pennies (30–50 per student) or other uniform-sized counters

Teacher Notes: The tubs should be large enough to hold at least two boats at a time. Larger tubs can accommodate two or three students and their boats at a time. Tubs should be filled with water high enough (5") to allow boats to turn on their sides and still sink completely.

Procedure

1. Prepare to test both boats to see which one can hold the most pennies.

Round 1

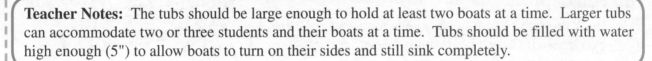

1. Predict how many pennies **Boat 1** will hold before sinking. Record this number on your *Boat Designs* recording sheet.

2. Place **Boat 1** in the tub of water and add one penny at a time until it sinks.

3. Record the number of pennies that **Boat 1** held before sinking on your *Boat Designs* recording sheet.

4. Was your prediction **greater than**, **less than**, or **equal to** the actual amount? Circle the correct symbol on your *Boat Design* recording sheet.

Round 2

1. Predict how many pennies **Boat 2** will hold before sinking. Record the number on your *Boat Designs* recording sheet.

2. Place **Boat 2** in the tub of water and add one penny at a time until it sinks.

3. Record the number of pennies that **Boat 2** held before sinking on your *Boat Designs* recording sheet.

4. Was your prediction **greater than**, **less than**, or **equal to** the actual amount? Circle the correct symbol on your *Boat Designs* recording sheet.

Round 3

1. Compare the results of the tests for **Boat 1** and **Boat 2**.

2. Which boat held the greatest amount of pennies? Fill in the answer on the bottom of your *Boat Designs* recording sheet.

3. Record the amount of pennies that this boat held on the class graph.

Buoyancy and Boat Design *(cont.)*

Culminating STEM Activities

1. Evaluate the graph to determine which boat held the most pennies (objects), and which held the fewest. Consider publishing a version of the graph on the computer.

2. Have a variety of boat-building materials and a scale available in a discovery center for further exploration (clay, wood, plastic, Styrofoam, paper, etc.)

   - Will another material build a stronger boat?

   - How much weight did each new boat hold? Use the scale to weigh the pennies or other small uniform-size counters. Record this information on a new class graph.

More					
50					
45					
40					
35					
30					
25					
20					
15					
10					
5					
	JO	LT	MJ	ST	RB

3. Send home the Family Connection letter (page 37) to be completed collaboratively. Later, create a class book using the Family Connection pages and each family's favorite boat.

4. Challenge another class to a contest to create a boat and experiment to see which boat holds the most objects.

5. Have students test the boat buoyancy experiment using found objects (both natural and manmade). For example: parts of plants (tree bark, leaves, branches), various containers, cooking items, toys, manipulatives, etc. What is the heaviest object a boat can hold? a rock? gravel?

6. Have students share what they discover about buoyancy when experimenting with various materials.

7. Invite a guest speaker into class to discuss boats, sailing, or working on a boat.

8. Find out more about different kinds of boats. Create a chart or collage and keep adding to it. Research which boats are the largest, carry the most weight, and travel the fastest.

9. Research and design boats built for speed rather than to carry weight. Try testing them using a fan to blow them across the water.

10. See if a boating field trip is possible.

Boat Designs

This is my design for **Boat 1:**

I predict Boat 1 will hold _____ objects before sinking.

The actual number of objects was _____.

My prediction was   **<   >   =**   the actual number of objects that **Boat 1** held before sinking.

This is my design for **Boat 2:**

I predict **Boat 2** will hold _____ objects before sinking.

The actual number of objects was _____.

My prediction was   **<   >   =**   the actual number of objects that **Boat 2** held before sinking.

The boat that held the greatest amount of objects was Boat _____.

Student's Name: _____

Date:_____

Hello,

We are investigating **BUOYANCY!** We each made two different-styled boats out of aluminum foil in project-based STEM activities to see which one could hold the most pennies without sinking.

Ask your child to tell you some of the facts that we have discovered about buoyancy and boat design.   Here are some questions to get your discussion started.

- What type of bottom helps a boat carry the most weight?

- Are flat-bottomed boats better for holding heavy things than V-shaped boat hulls?

Ask your child to explain how the design of the boat determines its purpose, whether it is designed for carrying heavy loads or for speed.

Please return this completed page so your child will be able to share your boat with our class.

Directions

1. Discuss different types of boats and choose the type of boat that your family likes best.
2. Draw the boat your family would like to have in the space below.
3. Think of a creative name for the boat, and print it on the line provided below.

_____

Exploring Color

STEM Objectives

1. Students will research colors and share information about primary and secondary colors, brown—a tertiary color, and hues and tints.

2. Students will observe colors and complete color mixing experiments using a variety of materials.

3. Data will be collected, recorded, and evaluated using charts, graphs, and/or spreadsheets.

Introduce the Topic – Colors

1. Read a nonfiction book about colors. Then discuss primary and secondary colors using appropriate vocabulary. (See page 40.)

2. Share nonfiction and fiction books about color. Discuss each book after it has been read and keep copies on display.

Suggestions

> *A Color of His Own* by Leo Lionni
>
> *A Rainbow of My Own* by Don Freeman
>
> *All The Colors of the Rainbow* by Allan Fowler
>
> *Color* by Kay Manolis
>
> *Color* by Maria Hidalgo
>
> *Color Dance* by Ann Jonas
>
> *Little Blue and Little Yellow* by Leo Lionni
>
> *Mouse Paint* by Ellen Stoll Walsh
>
> *White Rabbit's Color Book* by Alan Baker

3. Go online for additional information and check the websites on page 9.

Exploring Color *(cont.)*

Brainstorming Sessions

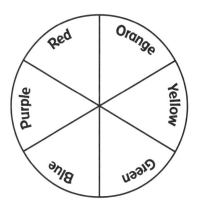

1. Ask students to identify the colors of the rainbow using a prism. Discuss the color spectrum and the order of the colors—*red, orange, yellow, green, blue, indigo,* and *violet.* Explain that indigo and violet are in the purple family and will be referred to as purple in the unit.

2. Work with students to complete a large color wheel utilizing the information. Post the color wheel to be used as a reference tool for students for subsequent experiments and when recreating their own color wheels. (See page 47.)

3. Create a list of questions to pose related to colors. Start with these:

   • How many colors are there? (Make a list and keep adding to it.)

   • Can you really create any color using only the primary colors?

   • Why aren't white or black in the rainbow?

   • Where can you find primary and secondary colors in nature? In the classroom?

Primary Colors in Nature		
Red	**Yellow**	**Blue**
rocks roses strawberries	sun daffodils pollen	sky water delphiniums hydrangeas

Primary Colors in the Classroom		
Red	**Yellow**	**Blue**
blocks markers	blocks chairs	blocks rug crayons

Color Vocabulary

A **rainbow** is an arc of colors appearing in the sky opposite the sun. A rainbow is formed when sunlight (which appears white) passes through raindrops. The raindrops act as prisms. The colors of a rainbow are always in the same order.

Red	Orange	Yellow	Green	Blue	Indigo	Violet

Black
White

Black is a color in which no light is reflected. When black is added to a color, it is called a **shade**.

White is the opposite of black. White reflects all colors. When white is added to a color it is called a **tint**.

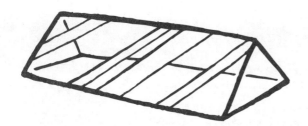

A **prism** is a transparent solid body, often having triangular ends (bases). It is used for dispersing light into a spectrum or for reflecting rays of light. Through a prism, we can see different colors. We can see all the colors of the rainbow because they are reflected in light.

The **primary colors** are red, yellow, and blue.   (Red) (Yellow) (Blue)

When two primary colors are mixed together, they create secondary colors.

 (Red) + (Yellow) = [Orange]   (Yellow) + (Blue) = [Green]   (Blue) + (Red) = [Purple]

The **secondary colors** are orange, green, and violet (purple).   [Orange] [Green] [Purple]

Brown is a **tertiary** color. It is made by mixing all three primary colors, a primary and a secondary color, or two secondary colors together.

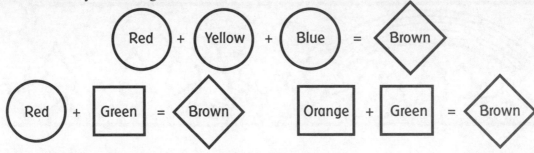

(Red) + (Yellow) + (Blue) = ⟨ Brown ⟩

(Red) + [Green] = ⟨ Brown ⟩   [Orange] + [Green] = ⟨ Brown ⟩

Exploring Color

The following project-based color activities are designed to encourage collaborative learning and discovery. Students should work in small groups (4 to 6). Encourage students to notice when they are using *science, technology, engineering*, or *math* during their color explorations.

Supplies

- 3 one-liter clear bottles of water
- clear mixing trays (or white Styrofoam egg cartons)
- clear plastic cups (8–12 oz.)
- clipboards (heavy cardboard with clothespins works well)
- food coloring or liquid water color (red, yellow, blue)
- pipettes, eye droppers, other similar tools
- prisms—various sizes and shapes
- small paintbrushes (1 per student)
- tempera paint (red, yellow, and blue)
- white daisies or carnations
- white coffee filters
- *Color Mixing* sheet (page 46)
- *Color Wheel* page (page 47)
- crayons, colored pencils, pencils
- hand-washing area, soap, water, and towels
- fiction and nonfiction books about color (See page 38 for suggestions.) and websites (See page 9.)

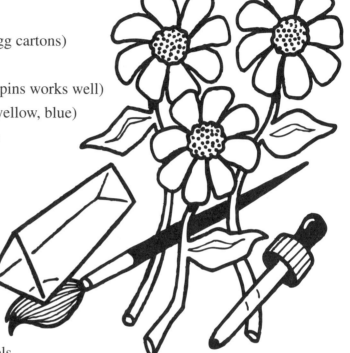

Teacher Preparation

1. Print out two *Color Mixing* sheets and one *Color Wheel* page for each student.

2. Prepare the three bottles of colored water, and have worksheets and other materials accessible for the demonstration.

3. Enlarge and color the *Color Vocabulary* page to serve as a guide. If possible, enlist student help.

4. Prepare the three Exploring Color stations and a Pipette Practice area (See page 42.) for student groups. Add additional materials, if appropriate. **Note:** If pipettes are not available, use eye droppers instead.

5. Plan on at least 10 minutes per station. Determine how and when students will rotate.

6. Consider creating charts, graphs, or spreadsheets to record group responses as part of the culminating events.

Exploring Color (cont.)

Student Preparation

1. Review the colors in the rainbow and the color wheel created during the brainstorming session.

2. Review the color vocabulary page or enlarged poster and display it near the stations.

3. Create large cards for each color of the rainbow. Add pictures of items or things in nature for the color. Pictures can be downloaded, drawn, or cut from magazines. Continually add to the color pages.

Introduce the Exploring Color Activities

1. Explain to students that they will be mixing a variety of colors using pipettes. While you are having your discussion, give each student a pipette to examine.

2. Demonstrate the tasks that are to be completed before having students break off into small groups.

3. Consider having Pipette Practice as a first station depending on the number and needs of your students. Make certain you identify which tool students will be using—pipettes or eye droppers.

4. Guide students with questions to encourage them to OBSERVE what they are doing.

5. Divide the class into small groups to complete the color experiments.

6. Encourage students to use the new vocabulary words when completing the experiments.

Pipette Practice

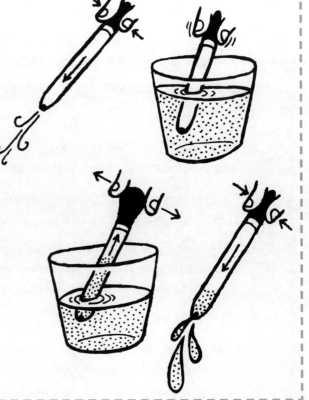

Step 1. Practice squeezing the bulb of the pipette.
"Do you feel or hear air rushing out?"

Step 2. Squeeze the bulb end of the pipette and place the pointed end in a container of water.
"Did all the water come out?"

Step 3. Slowly loosen the grip on the bulb letting water rise up into the pipette tube.
"Do bubbles form?"

Step 4. Hold the pipette filled with water over another container and slowly squeeze the pipette to let drops of water out.
"See if you can release one drop of water at a time. It takes practice!"

Exploring Color *(cont.)*

Station 1 – Primary Colors – *Science/Engineering/Math*

Tools

- 3 one-liter clear bottles of water
- *Color Mixing* sheet
- *Color Wheel* page
- crayons, colored pencils, pencils
- food coloring or liquid water color (red, yellow, blue)
- pipettes, eye droppers, other similar tools
- hand-washing area, soap, water, and towels

Procedure

1. Collaborate in your group. Predict how much coloring is needed to color one liter of water red.
2. Use pipettes to carefully measure and add the predicted amount of red coloring to the water.
3. Record how many drops of coloring were added to make the water red on the *Color Mixing* sheet.
4. Repeat the steps to make blue water using the second bottle.
5. Now, make yellow water using the third bottle.
6. Fill in the primary color sections on your *Color Wheel* page.

Note: These bottles of red, blue, and yellow water will be used for Stations 2 and 3.

Station 2 – Secondary Colors – *Science/Engineering/Math*

Tools

- clear mixing trays (or white Styrofoam egg cartons) for each pair of students
- clear plastic cups (8–12 oz.)
- *Color Wheel* page
- colored water in the primary colors (red, blue, yellow)
- crayons, pencils
- pipettes or eye droppers (at least one per cup)
- hand-washing area, soap, water, and towels

Procedure

1. Fill the three plastic cups 3/4 full. One will be red water, one will be blue water, and one will be yellow water.
2. Dip the end of a pipette into the red water and drop a few drops into one of the sections of the mixing tray.
3. Add drops from the blue water to the first one. What color did you make?
4. Record that color between the blue and red on your *Color Wheel* page.
5. Mix two more primary colors together using the pipette. What color did you make this time? Record it in the correct section of your *Color Wheel* page.
6. Look at your *Color Wheel* page to see which two colors you need to mix to make your final color.
7. Create your final color and add your results to the *Color Wheel* page. Compare your color wheel to others. Did everyone get the same results?

Exploring Color *(cont.)*

Station 3 – Free Color Exploration – *Science/Engineering/Math*
Tools

- clear mixing trays (or white Styrofoam egg cartons)
- *Color Mixing* sheet
- colored water in the primary colors (red, yellow, blue)
- crayons, colored pencils, pencils
- pipettes or eye droppers
- white coffee filters
- hand-washing area, soap, water, and towels
- newspaper or protective cloths

Procedure
Round 1

1. Explore color. Add the three primary colors—red, blue, and yellow—to the mixing trays.
2. Continue mixing colors in the trays, adding different amounts of each of the primary colors.
3. Continue to record the experiments on the *Color Mixing* sheets.
4. Use the pipettes to drop colored water onto the coffee filters. Watch as the colors blend. Are new colors created?
5. Let the coffee filters dry and recheck them to see if additional colors appeared.

Station 4 – Make a Flower Rainbow – *Science/Math*
Tools

- white daisies or carnations (one per student, plus 7 additional)
- 7 clear plastic cups or bud vases, labeled with one color of the rainbow
- red, yellow, blue water or food coloring and water

Procedure

1. Fill the cups with water. Each cup should be ¾ full.
2. Line up the 7 plastic cups in the order of the rainbow.
3. Mix colors as needed to fill each cup with the color water needed.
4. Place one flower in each cup.

Teacher Notes

1. Decide how to run this station based on time available and class size. Consider assigning each group one color of the rainbow to create.
2. Station 4 is best done at the end of the day since it takes hours for the stems and flowers to absorb the color. What a great surprise the next day or for Culminating STEM Activity #7.

Exploring Color *(cont.)*

Culminating STEM Activities

1. Ask each student to share one fact or discovery about his or her color experiments. Then, ask each student to identify a primary or secondary color on his or her clothes or in the room.

2. Extend the color-mixing activities. Challenge students to complete the following color experiments:

    *   Attempt to reproduce the color of an object like an apple or a piece of solid-colored fabric.

    *   Use tempera paints or watercolors to create brown, a tertiary color. Make a chart showing the different color combinations or recipes used to create brown. Review the color vocabulary page for hints.

3. Research the formation of rainbows (See page 9 for websites.) and experiment to create rainbows in the classroom or outdoors using a variety of materials (prisms, crystals, water, etc.).

4. Continue researching to answer the following questions:

    *   What are *complementary* colors?

    *   What colors are *warm* colors?

    *   What colors are *cool* colors?

    *   What colors are *neutral* colors?

Warm	Cool	Neutral
red	blue	black
yellow	purple	white
orange	green	gray

5. Use tempera paints to create tints and shades. (See page 40.) Create lists of shades and tints and the color recipes used to make them.

6. **Challenge:** What can you make or do with the colored coffee filters (Station 3) when they dry?

7. Ask each student to vote for his or her favorite color in the Flower Rainbow (Station 4). Allow student to "vote" by placing a white flower in the color water of their choice. Determine which color got the most votes. Graph the favorite colors.

8. Have a "Color Party Pot Luck" and ask students bring foods representing all the colors of the rainbow, or serve a rainbow fruit salad. Decorate with the coffee filter creations (#6) and the Flower Rainbow (#7).

9. Have students take pictures of the flowers and the coffee filters and create a display.

10. Send home the Family Connection page. (See page 48.)

Color Mixing

Directions: Use crayons to record the colors you mix in the boxes below. Use a pencil or felt pen to record the number of drops for each color on the line in front of the color spot. Remember to make a prediction to your partner or group before adding the newly created color. Share your color equations.

1	___ ▢ + ___ ▢ = ▭
2	___ ▢ + ___ ▢ = ▭
3	___ ▢ + ___ ▢ = ▭
4	___ ▢ + ___ ▢ = ▭
5	___ ▢ + ___ ▢ = ▭
6	___ ▢ + ___ ▢ = ▭
7	___ ▢ + ___ ▢ = ▭

Color Wheel

1. Complete **Station 1– Primary Colors** and **Station 2– Secondary Colors**. Then fill in the color wheel.

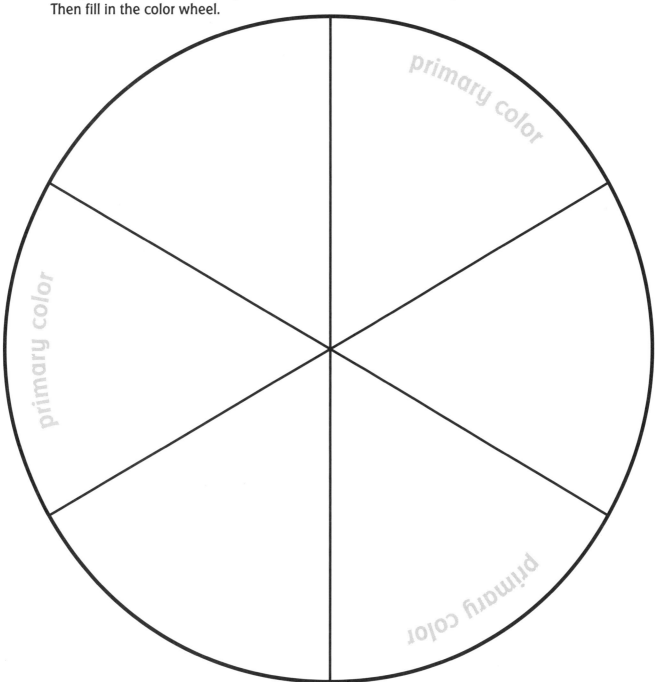

2. Find the complementary color on your wheel for each primary color. **Hint:** The complementary color is opposite the primary color.

red _____   blue _____   yellow _____

Student's Name: _____

Date:_____

Hello,

We are completing project-based STEM experiments with color! Your child has completed several color experiments and is learning about the color wheel. Ask your child to tell you the names of the **primary colors** (*red, blue,* and *yellow*) and **secondary colors** (*orange, green,* and *purple*).

If possible, allow your child to demonstrate what he or she has learned. You will need red, yellow, and blue food coloring. Mix the colors with your child to see what secondary and tertiary (brown) colors are produced.

Also, be on the lookout for rainbows!

Directions: Color the rainbow using the letter "clues" provided.

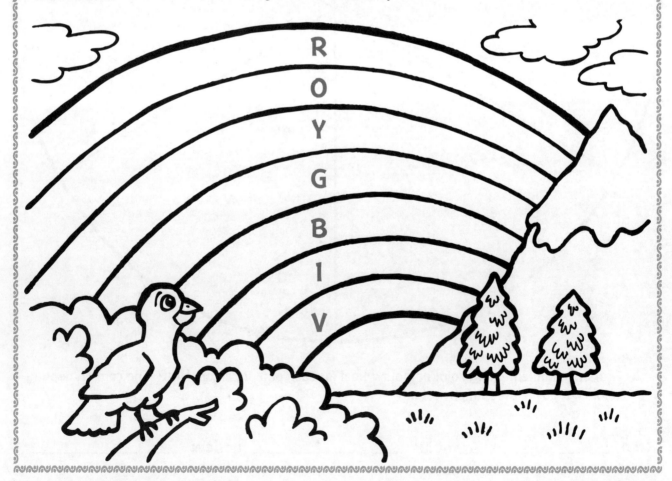

Discover Pumpkins

STEM Objectives

1. Students will research pumpkins and share information about life cycles and varieties.

2. Pumpkins and pumpkin seeds will be weighed, measured, and compared.

3. Pumpkin data will be collected, recorded, evaluated, and entered into charts, graphs, and/or spreadsheets.

Introduce the Topic – Pumpkins

1. Read a book about the life cycle of a pumpkin and discuss the life cycle using appropriate vocabulary. (See page 53.) Talk about germination, pollination, and harvesting. Practice sequencing the *Life Cycle of a Pumpkin* cards. (See pages 51–52.) If possible, laminate an enlarged set of cards for display.

2. Share nonfiction and fiction books about pumpkins. Discuss each book after it has been read, and keep copies in the classroom library or on display.

Suggestions

From Seed to Pumpkin by Wendy Pfeffer

How Many Seeds in a Pumpkin? by Margaret McNamara and G. Brian Karas

Life Cycle of a Pumpkin by Ron Fridell and Patricia Walsh

Pumpkin Circle: The Story of a Garden by George Levenson

Pumpkin, Pumpkin by Jane Titherington

Pumpkins by Ken Robbins

Seed, Sprout, Pumpkin, Pie (Picture the Seasons) by Jill Esbaum

The Biggest Pumpkin Ever by Steven Kroll

The Pumpkin Book by Gail Gibbons

3. Provide students with opportunities to go to online for additional information and check the websites on page 10. Seed catalogs and store advertisements are good for pictures, too.

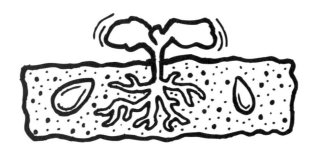

Discover Pumpkins *(cont.)*

Brainstorming Sessions

1. Ask students where pumpkins come from and guide them toward a discussion of how they grow.

2. Research various varieties of pumpkins and their attributes—*size, shape, color, mass, texture.* This research can be done as a whole class activity using an interactive whiteboard or by using seed catalogs or books.

3. Collaborate to create a chart or spreadsheet of different varieties (*Munchkin, Baby Bear, Aspen, Big Autumn,* etc.). Include a picture of each pumpkin researched and include the name of the pumpkin, its size, and color.

Munchkin	Baby Bear	Aspen	Big Autumn
mini	small	large	big
orange	orange	dark orange	yellow
all about the same size	flat; thin stem		

4. Compare and contrast the different pumpkins. Add to the chart as more varieties are discovered.

Life Cycle of a Pumpkin

1.	**pumpkin seed**

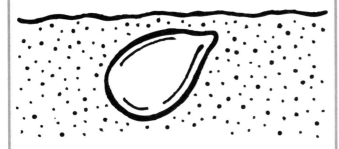

The seed is planted in the soil and needs sunshine and water to grow.

2.	**sprout**

The seed germinates, and a sprout emerges from the soil.

3.	**pumpkin vine and flower buds**

The sprout grows and forms a vine with leaves and flower buds.

4.	**male and female pumpkin flowers**

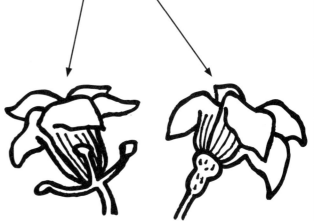

Every pumpkin needs a male flower and a female flower present at the same time.

Life Cycle of a Pumpkin *(cont.)*

5. **pollination**

Female flowers open about two weeks after the male flowers. Bees carry pollen from a male flower to a female flower to pollinate it.

6. **small pumpkin on bud**

A green pumpkin will begin to grow from the bud of the pollinated female flower.

7. **large pumpkin**

Once a pumpkin grows to its full size it turns orange and is ready to be harvested.

8. **pumpkin foods**

Pumpkin seeds and pumpkin foods can be prepared using parts of the pumpkin.

Pumpkin Vocabulary

A **pumpkin** is a gourd-like squash native to North America. It has a thick, orange or yellow shell that contains seeds and pulp.

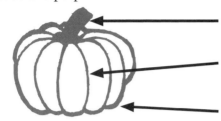

stem—the part of the pumpkin that is attached to the vine

ribs—indented ridges (creases) running from the top to the bottom of the pumpkin

skin—the thin, shiny, orange outer layer of a pumpkin

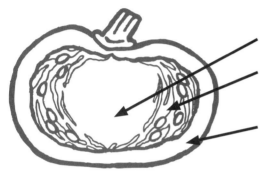

cavity—the empty, inside area of the pumpkin

fibrous strands—the slimy, mushy, mass of strings and seeds found inside the pumpkin cavity

pulp—the "meat" part of the pumpkin that is cooked to make tasty recipes and treats. To get to the pulp you must cut open the pumpkin, take out the seeds and strands, and peel the skin. What is left is the pulp.

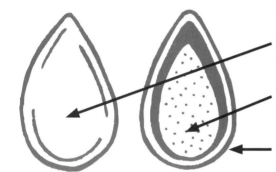

seed—a delicious and nutritious snack, or the beginning of next year's pumpkins

nut—located inside of the seed, it eventually develops into a new pumpkin

seed coat—also called a "seed jacket," the coat is the outer layer of the seed, protects the nut inside that will eventually emerge into a pumpkin plant

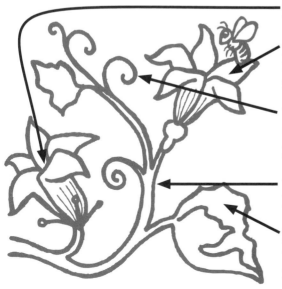

flower—the seed bearing part of the pumpkin plant

pollinate—the process by which pollen is transferred from a male flower to a female flower enabling fertilization and the growth of a pumpkin

tendrils—thin, hairlike "coils" that twist around objects on the ground to help anchor the pumpkin vine and protect it from blowing or breaking in the wind

vine—refers to the climbing or trailing nature of the stem, leaves, and tendrils of the pumpkin plant

leaf—the flat, green part attached to the pumpkin vine which absorbs energy from the sun for plant and fruit growth

Discover Pumpkins

The following project-based pumpkin activities are designed to encourage collaborative learning and discovery. Students should work in small groups (4 to 6). Encourage students to notice when they are using *science*, *technology*, *engineering*, or *math* during their pumpkin explorations.

Supplies

- pumpkins in a variety of colors and sizes (one per small group)
- 1 or 2 small kitchen scales (grams)
- 1 or 2 full-size scales (pounds)
- 1 or 2 balances
- measuring tapes, rulers, yardsticks, string
- cutting board and sharp knife
- crayons, colored pencils, pencils
- *Discover Pumpkins* journal (pages 59–60)
- paper plates, napkins, cups
- spoons, scrapers, containers (for pumpkin pulp and seeds)
- hand-washing area, soap and water, towels
- fiction and nonfiction books about pumpkins and pumpkin life cycles (See page 49 for suggestions.)
- pumpkin research websites (See page 10 for suggestions.)

Teacher Preparation

1. Provide a pumpkin with the top cut off for each small group (4–6 students). For safety reasons, an adult should do this prior to the activities. Have one or two extra pumpkins for demonstration and backup.

2. Print out and assemble a *Discover Pumpkins* journal for each student.

3. Prepare the five Discover Pumpkins stations for student groups. Add additional materials if appropriate. Copy and laminate each station card, and display it in the station.

4. Plan on at least 10 minutes per station. Determine how and when students will rotate.

5. Create charts, graphs, or spreadsheets as needed to record group responses and as part of the culminating events.

6. Arrange the pumpkins, journals, and writing implements near the stations.

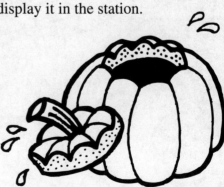

Discover Pumpkins *(cont.)*

Student Preparation

1. Review the life cycle of the pumpkin (pages 51–52). Enlist students to color an enlarged set of Pumpkin Life Cycle cards.

2. Display the Life Cycle cards.

3. Review pumpkin vocabulary words from the list on page 53. Create, illustrate, and display vocabulary word cards.

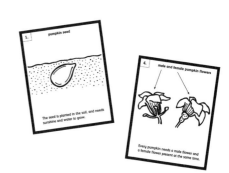

Introduce the *Discover Pumpkins* Activities

1. Divide the class into small groups to complete the activities at Station 1.

2. Stagger the starting times to allow each child to weigh a pumpkin (Station 1).

3. Demonstrate the tasks that are to be completed at each station before having students break off into small groups.

4. On the way to their first station, have students pick up their pumpkins and *Discover Pumpkins* journals. They will take their journals from station to station to record their findings.

5. Encourage students to use the new vocabulary words when completing the activities.

Station 1 – Weigh the Pumpkin – *Science/Engineering/Math*

Tools

- scales (pounds) or balances (grams)
- colored pencils, crayons, pencils
- *Discover Pumpkins* Journal

Procedure

1. Weigh the pumpkin. When you weigh a pumpkin, you are finding its **mass**.

2. Record the **mass** of the pumpkin on page 2 in the *Discover Pumpkins* journal.

Discover Pumpkins *(cont.)*

Station 2 – Observe and Draw Pumpkins – *Science/Engineering/Math*

Tools

- colored pencils, crayons, pencils
- pumpkins
- *Discover Pumpkins* Journals

Procedure

1. Observe the attributes of the pumpkin.

2. Draw a picture of the pumpkin on page 1 in the *Discover Pumpkins* journal.

3. Using the chart or spreadsheet created earlier, identify the variety of pumpkin and write its name in the journal on page 1.

4. Determine a method to count the number of ribs on the pumpkin. Record the number of ribs on page 2 in the journal.

Station 3 – Measure the Pumpkin's Circumference – *Science/Engineering/Math*

Tools

- measuring tapes, rulers, yardsticks, string
- colored pencils, crayons, pencils
- pumpkins
- *Discover Pumpkins* journals

Procedure

1. Figure out a way to measure the distance around the pumpkin. This distance is called the **circumference**. What tools will you use? (measuring tapes, rulers, yardsticks, string, or other?)

2. Measure the pumpkin (using inches) and record the circumference on page 2 in the *Discover Pumpkins* journal.

Discover Pumpkins *(cont.)*

Station 4 – Collect the Seeds – *Science/Technology/Engineering/Math*

Tools

- spoons, scrapers, etc.
- paper plates, cups, and napkins
- newspaper or table coverings
- hand-washing area

Procedure

1. Look at the array of tools (spoons, scrapers, etc).
2. Try different tools to remove the seeds. Don't forget your hands!
3. Carefully remove the seeds, strands, and pumpkin pulp from inside the pumpkin. Place the seeds on paper plates.
4. Determine the best way to get the seeds out.

   —Which tools worked the best—*spoons, scrapers, other?*

   —Did scooping from top to bottom work better than scooping from bottom to top?

Teacher Note: Save the seeds for Station 5 and for one of the culminating activities.

Station 5 – Estimate, Weigh, and Count Seeds – *Science/Technology/Engineering/Math*

Tools

- scales or balances
- paper cups and napkins
- hand-washing area
- pencils, crayons, colored pencils
- *Discover Pumpkins* journal

Procedure

1. Collaborate and design a method to measure out 20 grams of pumpkin seeds using a balance or a scale.
2. Estimate the amount of seeds in 20 grams. Record your estimate on page 3 in the *Discover Pumpkins* journal.
3. Measure out 20 grams of pumpkin seeds and place the pumpkin seeds in a cup.
4. Count the actual amount of seeds in 20 grams. Record the number of pumpkin seeds in 20 grams on page 3 in the *Discover Pumpkins* journal.
5. Compare the prediction to the actual count. Is the prediction **greater than**, **less than**, or **equal to** the actual number of pumpkin seeds? Circle the correct symbol on page 3 in the journal. Cross out the other two symbols.

Discover Pumpkins (cont.)

Culminating STEM Activities

1. Ask each student to share one fact or discovery about his or her pumpkin during group time.

2. Put finishing touches on the *Discovering Pumpkins* journals.

3. Poll students on their favorite pumpkin station. Graph their favorites.

   Station 1—Weigh the Pumpkin

   Station 2—Observe and Draw Pumpkins

   Station 3—Measure the Pumpkin's Circumference

   Station 4—Collect the Seeds

   Station 5—Estimate, Weigh, and Count Seeds

My Favorite Station				
	X	X		
	X	X		
X	X	X		X
X	X	X	X	X
1	**2**	**3**	**4**	**5**

4. Create a chart and vote on the best ways to remove seeds from a pumpkin.

5. Wash the remaining seeds in warm water to remove any stringy residue.

   —Devise methods to dry the seeds completely so that they do not mold.

   —How can you create a tray to dry them?

   —What might work faster—air, sun, or a hair dryer? **Note:** Drying time can take up to 2 weeks if air-drying is the chosen method.

6. When dry, count the seeds in groups of 10. Then count by tens to see how many seeds there were altogether.

7. Go online to find a recipe for pumpkin seeds and make them using a portion of the leftover seeds.

8. Send home the Family Connection letter (page 61) to be completed cooperatively by each student and his or her family. Share responses once they have been returned.

9. Try several types of pumpkin foods and vote on the favorite, or do some research and find and cook a pumpkin recipe to enjoy as a special treat.

Discover Pumpkins

Name: _____

This is a drawing of my pumpkin.

The variety I chose is _____.

(1)

My pumpkin has _____ ribs.

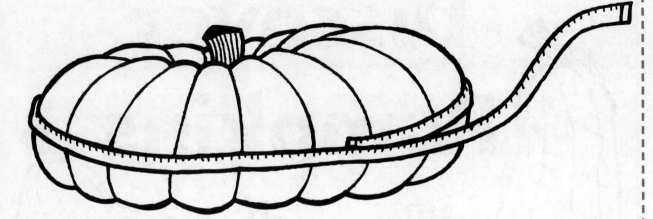

The pumpkin's **circumference** is _____ inches.

The **mass** of my pumpkin is _____. ②

I predict there will be _____ seeds in 20 grams of pumpkin seeds.

The actual amount of seeds is _____.

My prediction was >   <   =   the actual number of seeds. ③

Student's Name: _____

Date: _____

Hello,

Did you know a pumpkin is a fruit? A fruit is defined as being the part of the plant that contains seeds. The average pumpkin contains about a cup of seeds, so they are most definitely a fruit.

PUMPKINS come in a multitude of colors, shapes, and sizes. There are green, yellow, red, white, blue, and even multi-colored, striped pumpkins. They can be huge, tiny, fat, short, tall, round, pear-shaped, smooth, ribbed, and even warty. Some pumpkins are fabulous for culinary uses. Some pumpkins are more suited to being carved or displayed.

Today your child collaborated with classmates on a series of project-based STEM activities.

1. Please have him or her tell you about them. Here are some hints to help you ask questions.

    Science – explored the life cycle of pumpkins, including germination and pollination

    Technology – researched different kinds of pumpkins using a computer

    Engineering – determined ways to measure the pumpkin's circumference, and how to remove seeds from the cavity and dry them

    Math – weighed and measured pumpkins and counted seeds

2. Mention a few foods that you enjoy that have pumpkin as an ingredient.

Directions: Have your child choose his or her favorite pumpkin food, draw it, and fill in the blanks.

Two ingredients needed to make this food are:

_____

_____

My favorite pumpkin food is _____.

Healthy Hearts

STEM Objectives

1. Students will learn about the heart and the circulatory system.

2. Students will research, investigate, and experiment to find out how physical activity affects the rate of a person's heartbeat.

3. Students will plan and conduct a series of experiments to determine which types of activities increase a person's heartbeat.

4. Students will explain why physical activity affects the rate of a person's heartbeat.

5. Data will be collected, recorded, and evaluated using charts, graphs, and/or spreadsheets.

Introduce the Topic – Healthy Hearts

1. Read a nonfiction book about the circulatory system. Discuss the role of the heart in our circulatory system using appropriate vocabulary. (See page 64.)

2. Share nonfiction books about the circulatory system and physical activity. Discuss each book after it has been read, and keep copies on display.

Suggestions

The Amazing Circulatory System: How Does My Heart Work? by John Burstein

Get Moving (Sing and Read, Healthy Habits, K–2) by Jo Cleland

Get Up and Go! by Nancy Carlson

The Heart: Our Circulatory System by Seymour Simon

Let's Be Fit by P. K. Hallinan

My Amazing Body (A First Look at Health and Fitness) by Pat Thomas

The Magic School Bus Has a Heart by Ann Capeci and Joanna Cole

3. Provide opportunities for students to go online for additional information and check the suggested heart research websites provided on page 10.

Healthy Hearts *(cont.)*

Brainstorming Sessions

1. Help students list what they already know about the heart. Use pictures and props to facilitate the discussions.

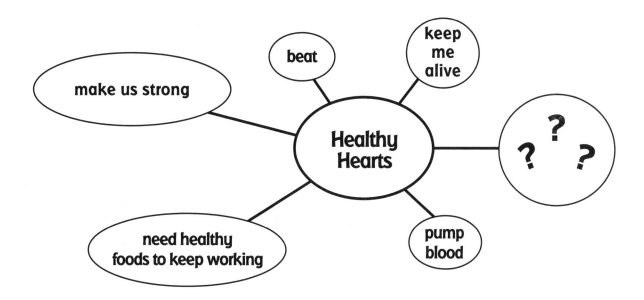

2. Create a list of questions to research and discuss related to the heart and the circulatory system. Start with these:

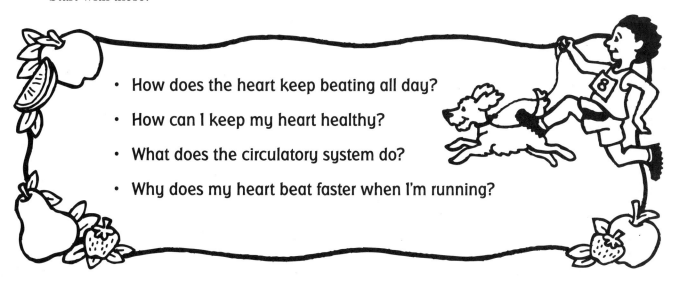

- How does the heart keep beating all day?
- How can I keep my heart healthy?
- What does the circulatory system do?
- Why does my heart beat faster when I'm running?

Healthy Heart Vocabulary

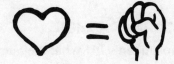

The **heart** is a muscle about the size of a fist. The heart acts like a pump and its job is to pump clean blood (and food for cells) throughout the body. The heart is always working, even when a person is sleeping.

The heart pumps cleaned blood filled with oxygen throughout the body through tubes called **arteries**.

"Used" blood filled with carbon dioxide and other things the body doesn't need is pumped back to the heart. The blood that traveled away from the heart through the **arteries** travels back to the heart through another set of tubes called **veins**.

When you listen to your **heartbeat** you are listening to the **valves** (doors) letting blood in from tubes called **veins** and out through tubes called **arteries**.

The heart sends the used blood to the lungs. We know **lungs** help us breathe. When we inhale, our lungs fill up with air (oxygen). When we exhale, our lungs let the air out (carbon dioxide).

So where does the carbon dioxide we breathe out come from? Lungs collect carbon dioxide picked up by our blood while traveling back to the heart. The lungs and heart work together to put in the new, fresh oxygen we breathed in (inhaled). Then the blood starts back around our bodies again!

The heart, lungs, arteries, and veins are part of a system called the **circulatory system**.

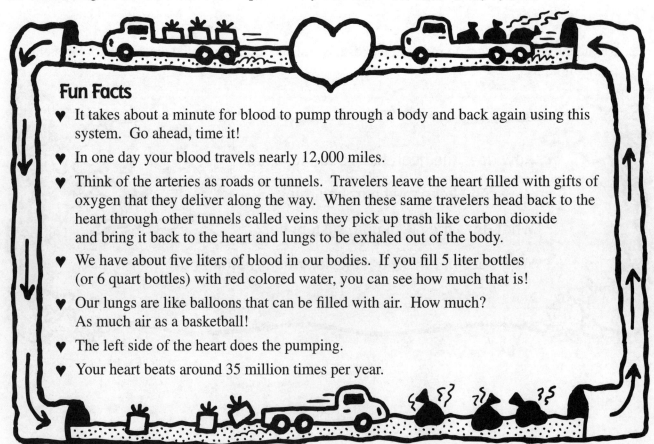

Fun Facts

- ♥ It takes about a minute for blood to pump through a body and back again using this system. Go ahead, time it!
- ♥ In one day your blood travels nearly 12,000 miles.
- ♥ Think of the arteries as roads or tunnels. Travelers leave the heart filled with gifts of oxygen that they deliver along the way. When these same travelers head back to the heart through other tunnels called veins they pick up trash like carbon dioxide and bring it back to the heart and lungs to be exhaled out of the body.
- ♥ We have about five liters of blood in our bodies. If you fill 5 liter bottles (or 6 quart bottles) with red colored water, you can see how much that is!
- ♥ Our lungs are like balloons that can be filled with air. How much? As much air as a basketball!
- ♥ The left side of the heart does the pumping.
- ♥ Your heart beats around 35 million times per year.

Circulatory System

Directions

1. Label the heart and lungs.

2. Use a red marker or crayon to trace the dashed lines. They are the **arteries**.

3. Use a blue marker or crayon to trace the dotted lines. They are the **veins**.

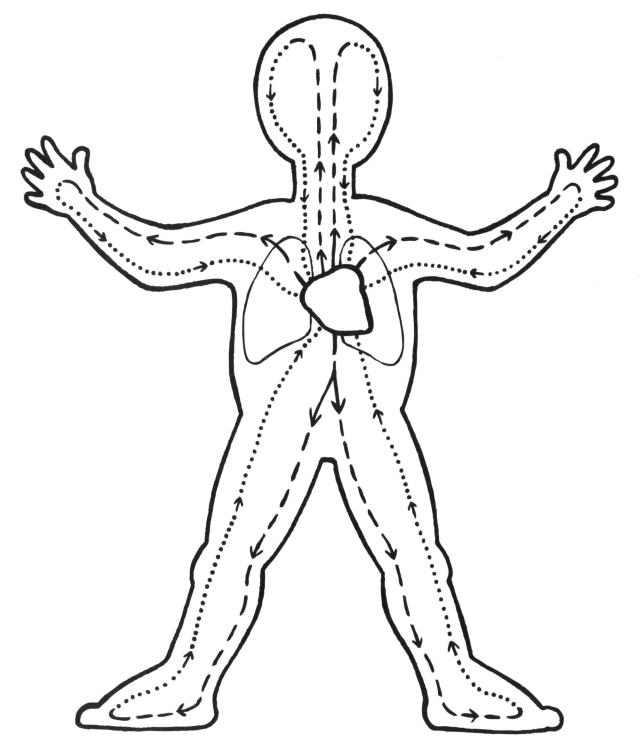

Healthy Hearts

The following project-based activities about the healthy heart are designed to encourage collaborative learning and discovery. Students can work independently or in small groups (3 to 4) depending on the setup for each activity. Encourage students to notice when they are using *science, technology, engineering*, or *math* during their Healthy Hearts experiments.

Supplies

- 1-minute timer
- 5 clear plastic 1-liter bottles
- balloons
- basketball
- butcher paper (for two large graphs)
- clear plastic cups (one per student)
- disinfecting wipes (one per student)
- *Circulatory System* diagram (page 65)
- *Healthy Hearts* recording sheet (page 71)
- Human Circulatory System poster (optional)
- red food coloring
- red fruit juice (one box for each student)
- stethoscopes (at least one per small group)
- stopwatches (at least one per small group)
- nonfiction books about the heart and the circulatory system (See page 62 for suggestions.)
- heart research websites (See page 10 for suggestions.)

Teacher Preparation

1. Print copies of the *Healthy Hearts* recording sheet and the *Circulatory System* diagram for each student.

2. Familiarize yourself with the concepts of the circulatory system and how the heart pumps the blood throughout the body.

3. Set up a series of props including a 1-minute timer, a basketball, five 1-liter bottles filled with red water, and some balloons. Use these items to illustrate the Fun Facts on the vocabulary page. Encourage students to include them in their own demonstrations.

4. Display pictures or posters of the human circulatory system for the students to refer to.

5. Create three graphs so that each student can record the number of heartbeats they counted after they had finished resting, walking, and 25 jumping jacks.

6. Create additional charts, graphs, or spreadsheets as needed to record group responses and as part of the culminating events.

7. Arrange areas (stations) where students can experiment, record, and graph their data.

Healthy Hearts *(cont.)*

Student Preparation

1. Review the heart and circulatory system information from the brainstorming sessions. Has any new information been discovered that can be added to the charts or displays?

2. Try this. Cover a table. Give each student a juice box and a cup. Explain that the juice box is the heart and the straw is an artery. The cup can be the body. Each student will put his or her straw in the box and squeeze the box so that the juice goes into the straw to the cup. Explain that the squeezing motion is a lot like the heart pumping blood into the arteries of our bodies. **Note:** The pressure needed to squeeze a tennis ball is more accurate in terms of how hard the heart squeezes to pump.

3. Practice finding your heart and feeling the beats. Be very quiet....Hold your hand on your chest. Move your hand a little to the left. Can you feel your heart beating? Listen. Do you hear it?

Introduce the Healthy Hearts Activities

1. Divide the students into small groups to complete their Healthy Hearts experiments. Determine how many students can be in each station at a time.

2. Explain that each student will be conducting experiments to determine the effect of physical activity (exercise) on the rate of each individual's heartbeat.

3. Share a stethoscope with the class and ask if anyone knows what it is for. Discuss the instrument and how it is used to listen to a heartbeat. Model how to use the stethoscope safely—speak quietly when using it. Remind students that they will need to clean the earpieces of the stethoscope with the disinfectant wipes after each use.

   Teacher Tip: When the student has the stethoscope earpieces in his or her ears, place the round receptor piece on the student's chest. Holding it with your fingers, you can feel the heartbeat and help the student to count accurately.

4. Distribute the *Healthy Hearts* recording sheets. Encourage students to refer back to their resources as needed and to use the new vocabulary words when completing the experiments.

5. Explain how students will move from one physical activity to the next and where to record their data on the class graphs. Do a few jumping jacks together to make certain all know how.

6. Have a student demonstrate the steps of the experiment: predict a heartbeat, perform the physical activity, listen and count your heartbeat using a stethoscope, and record your findings on a *Healthy Hearts* recording sheet.

Healthy Hearts *(cont.)*

Using a Stethoscope

1. Carefully place the earpieces in your ears.

2. Hold the round (receptor) piece over your heart.

3. Listen to the sound of your heartbeat. Thump! Thump!

4. Clean the earpieces when you are done.

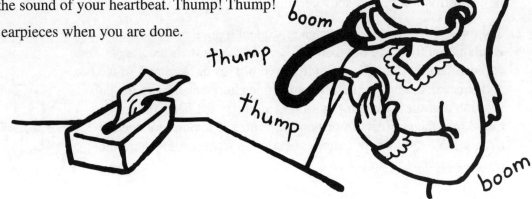

Safety Note: A stethoscope is a tool, not a toy. Treat it carefully. Do not yell into the receptor piece when someone is wearing the stethoscope. It could damage their ears.

Station 1 – Healthy Hearts: Resting – *Science/Technology/Engineering/Math*

Tools

- nonfiction books, posters, and pictures about the circulatory system and heart
- *Healthy Hearts* recording sheet (for each student)
- stopwatch, or watch with second hand
- stethoscope
- disinfectant wipes
- timer (for 5 minutes)
- pencils

Procedure

1. Sit with a partner and write your names on your *Healthy Hearts* recording sheets.

2. Set the timer for 5 minutes.

3. Predict how many times your heart will beat in 10 seconds after sitting for 5 minutes. Look at the books and posters or sit somewhere restful while you wait quietly until the timer goes off. Record your predictions.

4. Take turns using the stethoscope. Listen and count your heartbeats for 10 seconds. Your partner will time you using a stopwatch or watch with a second hand. Then switch.

5. Record the actual number of heartbeats you heard. Circle whether your prediction was **<, >,** or **=** the actual number of heartbeats in 10 seconds while resting.

Healthy Hearts *(cont.)*

Station 2 – Healthy Hearts: Walking – *Science/Technology/Engineering/Math*

Tools

- *Healthy Hearts* recording sheet (for each student)
- stopwatch, or watch with second hand
- stethoscope
- disinfectant wipes
- timer (for 5 minutes)
- pencils

Procedure

1. You will count your heartbeats after walking for 5 minutes.
2. Predict how many times your heart will beat in 10 seconds after walking. Record your predictions.
3. Set the timer for 5 minutes.
4. Walk for 5 minutes.
5. Take turns using the stethoscope. Listen and count your heartbeats for 10 seconds. Your partner will time you using a stopwatch or watch with a second hand. Then switch.
6. Record the actual number of heartbeats you heard. Circle whether your prediction was **< >** or **=** the actual number of heartbeats in 10 seconds after walking for 5 minutes.

Station 3 – Healthy Hearts: Jumping Jacks – *Science/Technology/Engineering/Math*

Tools

- *Healthy Hearts* recording sheet (for each student)
- stopwatch, or watch with second hand
- stethoscope
- disinfectant wipes
- timer (for 5 minutes)
- pencils

Procedure

1. You will count your heartbeats after doing 25 jumping jacks.
2. Predict how many times your heart will beat in 10 seconds after doing the jumping jacks. Record your predictions.
3. Take turns using the stethoscope. Listen and count your heartbeats for 10 seconds. Your partner will time you using a stopwatch or watch with a second hand. Then switch.
4. Record the actual number of heartbeats you heard. Circle whether your prediction was **<, >,** or **=** the actual number of heartbeats in 10 seconds after doing 25 jumping jacks.

Healthy Hearts (cont.)

Culminating STEM Activities

1. Post three graphs, one labeled *Healthy Heart: Resting*, one labeled *Healthy Heart: Walking*, and one for *Healthy Heart: Jumping Jacks*.

   —Ask each student to use the information on his or her recording sheets to fill in the graphs.

   —Then, as a group, evaluate the graphs to determine the affect of physical activity on the heart.

2. Have the students try other physical activities to complete this experiment. Provide time to research healthy heart activities online (See page 10.) and from other sources.

   —Generate a list of 3 different forms of exercise (e.g., dancing, rolling on a mat, running).

   —Use the stations to test the 3 new forms of exercise.

   —Create additional graphs for the new exercises. Which one gets the heart rate going the most?

3. Compare the results of the chosen activities with the information on the charts. See what other comparisons students can make.

   • What types of activities will increase your heart rate?

   • Why does your heart rate increase when you exercise?

   • What about laying down compared to sitting and reading? Is there a difference in heart rate?

4. Arrange all the graphs in order in the room from *least* amount of activity (heartbeats) to the *greatest*.

5. Complete the *Circulatory System* diagram (page 65). Label the **heart**, **lungs**, **veins**, and **arteries**.

6. Send home the Family Connection activity (page 72) to be completed collaboratively. Have students share their families' Healthy Hearts tip when the pages are returned. Create a list of tips that could be done in class.

7. Get up and stretch! What could students do every day in class for five minutes to add a little exercise? Have the students develop a plan to exercise daily and create a class book. Perhaps the leader each day can pick an activity.

8. Invite a guest speaker into class to discuss maintaining a healthy heart and ways they can eat healthy and exercise daily.

9. Film students doing different "five-minute" activities. Share with parents.

Healthy Hearts

I predict that my heart will beat _____ times in 10 seconds after **sitting** for 5 minutes.

I counted _____ heartbeats in 10 seconds.

My prediction was   <   >   =   the actual number of heartbeats I counted.

I predict that my heart will beat _____ times in 10 seconds after **walking** for 5 minutes.

I counted _____ heartbeats in 10 seconds.

My prediction was   <   >   =   the actual number of heartbeats I counted.

I predict that my heart will beat _____ times in 10 seconds after **doing 25 jumping jacks**.

I counted _____ heartbeats in 10 seconds.

My prediction was   <   >   =   the actual number of heartbeats I counted.

Student's Name: _____

Date:_____

Hello,

We have been studying how to keep our hearts healthy. Your child has completed research about the **HEART** and the **CIRCULATORY SYSTEM** and conducted project-based STEM experiments to see how physical activity affects his or her heartbeat.

Please ask your child to tell you some of the facts that we have discovered about the heart and circulatory system. Here are a few questions to get your conversation started.

♥ What part of the body works like a pump? *(heart)* What does it pump? *(blood)*

♥ What parts of the body are like tubes or tunnels? *(arteries and veins)* What do they do?

♥ How does exercise help our hearts stay healthy?

Directions: Discuss the importance of staying healthy with your child.   Decide on one way that your family can work to keep your hearts healthy. Return this completed page to class.

Here is a drawing of my family's Healthy Hearts tip:

We can keep our hearts healthy by _____

_____

Spiders

STEM Objectives

1. Students will conduct research and share information about spiders.

2. Students will create models of different types of spiders and their webs.

3. Spider data will be collected, recorded, and evaluated using charts, graphs, and/or spreadsheets.

Introduce the Topic – Spiders

1. Read a nonfiction book about spiders. Then discuss characteristics of spiders and their webs to introduce appropriate vocabulary. (See page 75.)

2. Share nonfiction and fiction books about spiders. Discuss each book after it has been read, and keep copies on display.

Suggestions

Are You a Spider? (Backyard Books)
by Judy Allen and Tudor Humphries

Be Nice to Spiders by Margaret Bloy Graham

National Geographic Readers: Spiders
by Laura Marsh

Spiders by Gail Gibbons

Spiders by Seymour Simon

Spiders (Eye to Eye with Animals) by Don McLeese

Spiders' Secrets (DK Readers) by Richard Platt

Spinning Spiders (Let's-Read-and-Find-Out Science 2)
by Melvin Berger

The Very Busy Spider by Eric Carle

Time For Kids: Spiders!
by the Editors of TIME For Kids

3. Provide opportunities for students to go online for additional information and check the suggested spider websites on page 11.

Spiders (cont.)

Brainstorming Sessions

1. Help students list what they already know about spiders (fact and fiction).

2. Create a Venn diagram comparing spiders (arachnids) to insects.

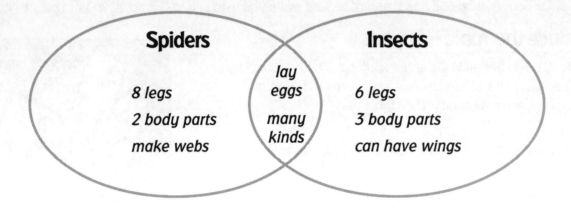

Spiders

8 legs

2 body parts

make webs

lay eggs

many kinds

Insects

6 legs

3 body parts

can have wings

3. Create a list of questions related to spiders to discuss.

   Start with these:

   - How many different types of spiders are there?
   - Do spiders hurt people?
   - What types of spiders are dangerous?
   - Do all spiders make the same type of web?
   - How do spiders help our environment?

Spider Vocabulary

A spider is an **arachnid**.

A spider has two main body parts—the head and the abdomen.

The **head** (*cephalothorax*) is the first of the two spider body parts.

The head has two sensory feelers (**pedipalps**), two fangs, and compound eyes. This body part also includes the eight legs.

Interesting Fact: If a spider leg is lost, a new one will grow in its place.

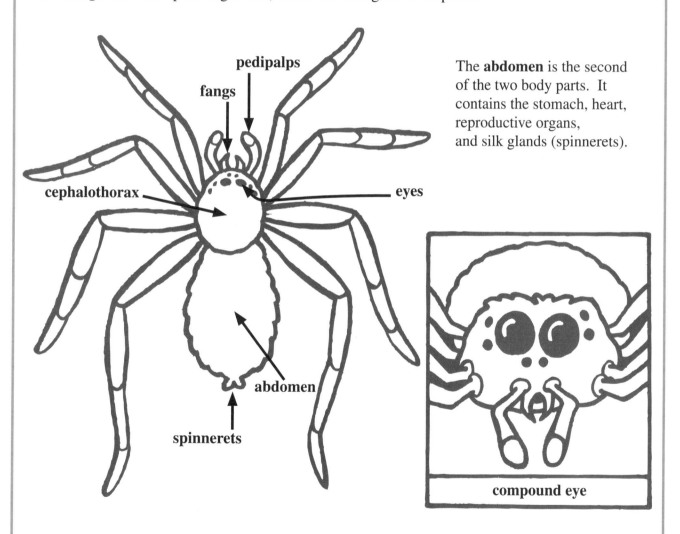

The **abdomen** is the second of the two body parts. It contains the stomach, heart, reproductive organs, and silk glands (spinnerets).

The **spinnerets** are at the end of the abdomen. They produce silk to build webs to catch insects, to make egg cases, and to catch the wind to fly (ballooning). Most spiders have six spinnerets.

Types of Spider Webs

A **web** is spun by a spider to trap prey. Webs trap insects including flies, crickets, mosquitoes, beetles, butterflies, and bees. Each type of spider has its own type of web. Here are four examples:

Orb Web—a circular spider web

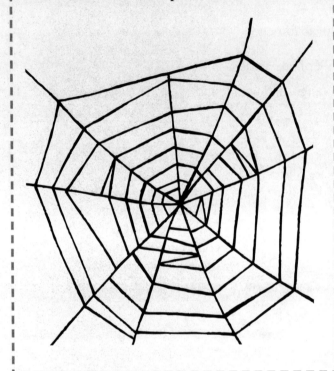

Triangle Web—a triangular-shaped spider web

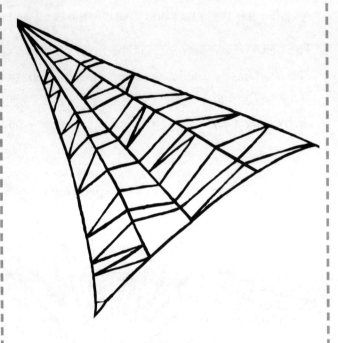

Sheet Web—an irregular spider web woven in a single plane and looking like a flattened hammock

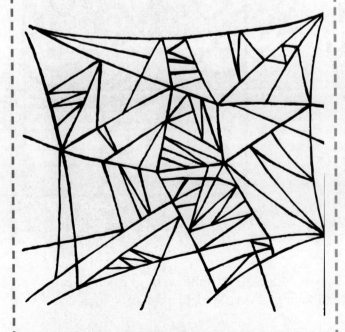

Funnel Web—a funnel-shaped spider web; the funnel-web spider perches in the center of the web

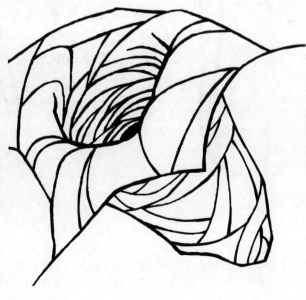

Spiders

The following project-based spider activities are designed to encourage collaborative learning and discovery. Students should work in small groups (4 to 6). Encourage students to notice when they are using s*cience, technology, engineering,* or *math* during their spider explorations.

Supplies

- 2" pom poms* (1 or 2 per student)
- 1½" pom poms* (1 or 2 per student)
- chenille stems* (4 per student in spider colors)
- black construction paper (one 9" x 12" sheet per student)
- white chalk, white fabric paint, or white gel pens
- white yarn (15" per student)
- Tacky Glue®
- scissors, hole punches
- white construction paper (1" square per student)
- fine-tipped markers, permanent markers
- *Spider Fact Sheet* (page 81)
- hand-washing area, soap, water, and towels
- nonfiction and fiction books about spiders (See page 73 for suggestions.)
- spider research websites (See page 11 for suggestions.)

* Note: Provide "spider" colors such as brown, black, white, red, yellow, green, and gray.

Teacher Preparation

1. Print out a *Spiders Fact Sheet* for each student.

2. Familiarize yourself with the characteristics of spiders and their webs to better guide the discussions. If possible, enlarge the illustrated Spider Vocabulary page and the Webs page.

3. Display examples and pictures of several types of webs and spiders for the students to refer to during the activities.

4. Create charts, graphs, or spreadsheets as needed to record group responses and as part of the culminating events.

5. Arrange areas (stations) where students can research, write, and create their spider models and webs.

RESEARCH   WRITE   CREATE

Spiders *(cont.)*

Student Preparation

1. Review the characteristics of spiders and their webs and other information from the brainstorming sessions. Ask if any new information has been discovered that can be added to the chart.

2. Discuss the enlarged version of the Spider Vocabulary page and then display it. If an enlarged copy of the vocabulary page is unavailable, ask students to create illustrated vocabulary word cards.

Introduce the *Spiders* Activities

1. Divide the students into small groups to complete their spider activities.

2. Explain that each student will choose a spider and make a model of the spider and its web.

3. Outline the process of choosing a type of spider for a model and how to research the type of web it spins. Establish Station 1 at a table near the computer.

4. Model how to print the spider's name and the type of web on the *Spider Fact Sheet* page. Explain that the fact sheet will be displayed with the finished spider model and web.

5. Distribute the *Spider Fact Sheet* to each student. Encourage students to refer back to their resources as needed and to use the new vocabulary words when completing the activities.

6. Explain how to proceed at each work area. Model how to use the materials. Remind students that they are creating scientific models— accuracy is important.

Station 1 – Spider and Web Research – *Science/Technology/Engineering/Math*

Tools

- nonfiction books, posters, and pictures about spiders and webs
- access to approved websites (See page 11.)
- pencils, colored pencils, fine-tipped markers, crayons
- *Spider Fact Sheet* (for each student)

Procedure

1. Look through several books about spider's and research online.

2. Choose a spider and record the spider's name on your fact sheet.

3. Find out how many eyes your spider has.

4. Identify which type of web your spider spins (if it spins a web at all). Add the information to the fact sheet.

5. Illustrate your spider and its web on the fact sheet. Be as accurate as you can.

Spiders *(cont.)*

Station 2 – Spider Model – *Science/Technology/Engineering/Math*

Tools

- pom poms (1½" and 2" for each student)
  —brown, black, white, red, yellow, green, gray
- chenille stems (4 per student in spider colors)
- Tacky Glue and scissors
- black fine-tipped markers
- white construction paper (1" square per student)
- *Spider Fact Sheet*
- nonfiction books and pictures of spiders

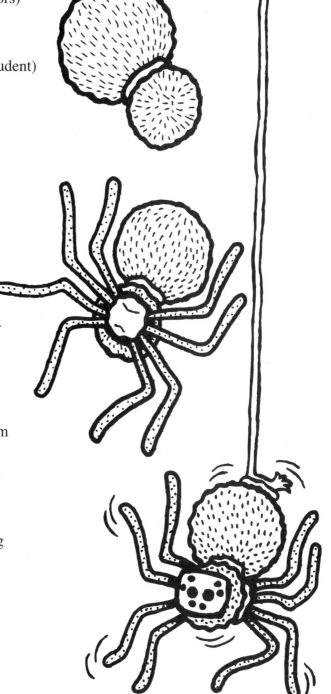

Procedure

1. Use your *Spider Fact Sheet* and other available books and pictures as guides for your spider model.

2. Choose 2 pom poms and 4 chenille stems to match your spider.

3. Use one pom pom for the head and another pom pom for the body (abdomen). Attach the pom poms to each other using glue. Let them dry.

4. Fold the 4 chenille stems in half. Twist them together to form 8 spider legs.

5. Glue the legs to the bottom of the pom pom representing the head *(cephalothorax)*.

6. Trim the 1" square to make an oval for the compound eyes. Use a felt-tipped-marker to draw the correct number of eyes.

7. Glue the eyes to the pom pom representing the head.

8. Add details to your spider.

Spiders

Station 3 – Spider Webs – *Science/Technology/Engineering/Math*

Tools

- nonfiction books and pictures of spiders
- computer access to approved websites
- black construction paper (9" x 12" sheet per student)
- white chalk, white fabric paint, or white gel pens
- white yarn (15" per student)
- *Spider Fact Sheet*
- completed spider from Station 2.

Procedure

1. Use your *Spider Fact Sheet* and other available books and pictures as guides for your spider web model.

2. Take one piece of black construction paper and choose which type of media (chalk, gel pen, fabric paint) you will use to create your spider's web on the paper.

3. Create the web and let it dry.

4. Tie the yarn around one of your spider's legs.

5. Attach the other end of the yarn to the top of your web.

6. The spider should be able to be moved around the web.

Culminating STEM Activities

1. Ask each student to share the name of his or her spider and the type of spider's web.

2. Plan for a "Spider Model Day" and invite families or another class to come in and view the spider models and webs. Download pictures of each spider to add to the displays.

3. Put finishing touches on the *Spider Fact Sheets*.

4. Send home the Family Connection letter (page 82) to complete collaboratively at home. Share the results when the pages are returned.

5. Go on a nature walk and see if students can discover any spiders or spider webs. Look high and low. Observe closely, but do not touch! Film or photograph discoveries.

6. Bring in a tarantula or other large spider to observe in the classroom.

Spider Fact Sheet

My spider is called _____.

This spider has eyes _____.

This spider spins _____web.

Student's Name: _____

Date:_____

Hello,

We are completing project-based STEM activities about **SPIDERS!** Your child has completed several activities and is learning more and more about spiders. Ask your child to tell you some of the interesting facts that we have discovered about spiders. Did you know....

1. Spiders are NOT insects! Spiders have 2 body parts and 8 legs, while insects have 3 body parts and 6 legs.

2. Some spiders spin webs and some live under ground.

Directions: Work together and label the spider. Use the word bank.

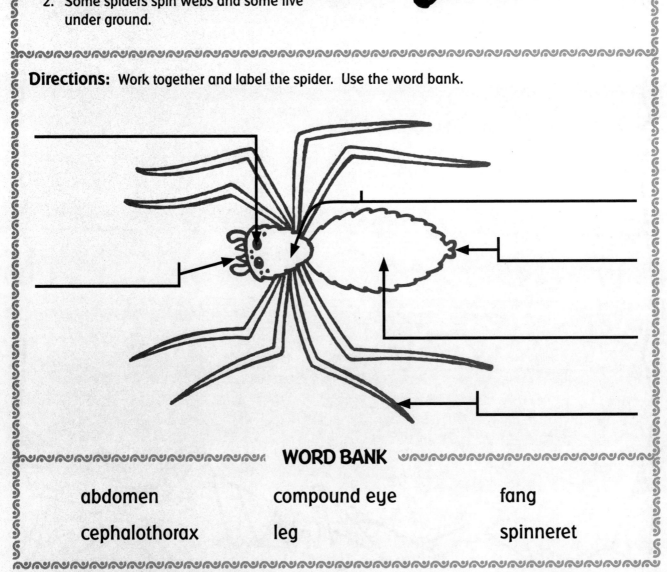

WORD BANK

abdomen	compound eye	fang
cephalothorax	leg	spinneret

Static Electricity

STEM Objectives

1. Students will research and share information about static electricity.

2. Four static electricity experiments will be completed using a variety of household materials.

3. Data will be collected, recorded, and evaluated using charts, graphs, and/or spreadsheets.

Introduce the Topic – Static Electricity

1. Read a nonfiction book about static electricity and discuss the facts presented in the book using appropriate vocabulary. (See page 85.)

2. Share nonfiction and fiction books about electricity throughout the unit. Discuss each book after it has been read and keep copies on display.

Suggestions

All About Electricity by Melvin Berger

Awesome Experiments for Curious Kids: Electricity and Magnetism, Forces, Plants and Living Things, Heat, Materials, Light and Sound by Trevor Cook and Sally Henry

Awesome Experiments in Electricity & Magnetism by Michael A. DiSpezio

Charged Up: The Story of Electricity (Science Works) by Jacqui Bailey

DK Eyewitness Books: Electricity by Steve Parker and Laura Buller

Switch On, Switch Off (Let's-Read-and-Find-Out Science 2) by Melvin Berger and Carolyn Croll

The Magic School Bus and the Electric Field Trip by Joanna Cole and Bruce Degen

Zap! It's Electricity (My Science Library) by Buffy Silverman

3. Provide opportunities for students to go online for additional information and check the suggested static electricity websites on page 11.

Static Electricity *(cont.)*

Brainstorming Sessions

1. Pose the question, "What is electricity?" When we think of electricity, light or light bulbs might come to mind. We might also think of the current that comes into our homes for heat, lighting, and appliances. We can't see the current (energy from batteries or generators), we just know it is there when we flip a switch or press a button. Add ideas to a donut web.

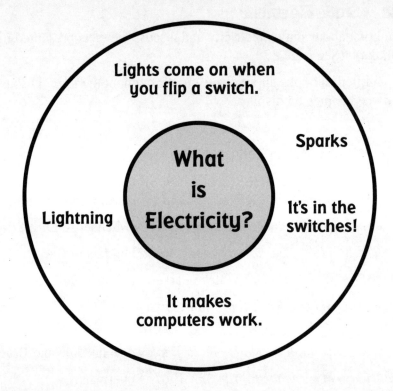

2. After a discussion about electricity, ask what they know about "static" electricity. Help students create another donut web listing all the facts they know about static electricity.

3. Ask open-ended questions regarding static electricity. The following questions or prompts should get students thinking:

   • Why does your hair stand straight up sometimes when you take off a hat or pull a sweater over your head?

   • Why do you get a "shock" sometimes when you touch a metal object after walking across a carpet?

   • Have you ever noticed static electricity when folding laundry? What happens to the clothes?

   • Why are some materials attracted and others repelled?

Add student responses to the donut webs.

Static Electricity Vocabulary

Electricity is related to charged particles. All matter (materials) is made up of atoms which contain tiny particles called protons and electrons. Matter can have positive or negative charged particles.

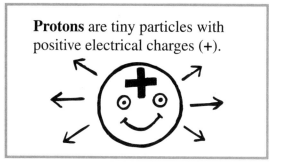

Protons are tiny particles with positive electrical charges (+).

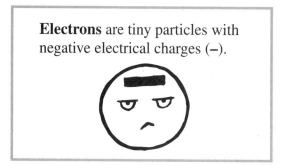

Electrons are tiny particles with negative electrical charges (−).

Materials with like charges move away (repel) from each other, those with opposite charges move near (attract) each other.

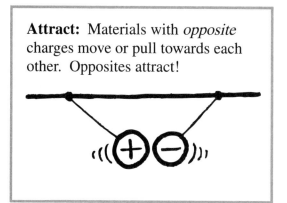

Attract: Materials with *opposite* charges move or pull towards each other. Opposites attract!

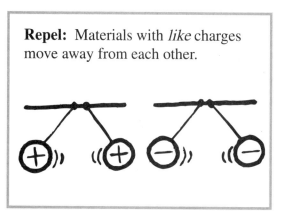

Repel: Materials with *like* charges move away from each other.

Protons and electrons usually balance each other. But, sometimes when two surfaces rub together (friction), some of the electrons rub off one surface and attach to the other. This creates an imbalance of electrons and THAT causes static electricity. Static electricity means "non-moving" electricity. Think of a sock stuck to a shirt—it isn't moving. The sock picks up more electrons and is no longer balanced.

How Static Electricity Works: When you rub a balloon on your hair, the electrons from each hair jump onto the balloon leaving each individual hair positively charged. The balloon is negatively charged, and since your hair is positively charged, your hair and the balloon are attracted to each other. Since "like" charges move away from each other, each positively-charged hair is trying to move away from another positively-charged hair and ends up standing straight up.

Static Electricity

The following project-based static electricity activities are designed to encourage collaborative learning and discovery. Students should work in pairs. Encourage students to notice when they are using *science, technology, engineering,* or *math* during their static electricity explorations.

Supplies

- wool or acrylic socks (**Note:** Cotton socks are not as effective.)
- Styrofoam pieces (beads from beanbags, packing peanuts)
- 9" or 11" balloons (inflated and tied by students)
- large trays or cookie sheets with edges
- empty soda cans
- *Static Electricity* journal pages (pages 91–92)
- string (cut in 18" lengths)
- timer (10–15 seconds)
- yardstick or meter stick
- measuring tape
- crayons, colored pencils, pencils, scissors
- nonfiction books about static electricity (See page 83 for suggestions.)
- cold water source (a continuous stream of water, preferably from a faucet)
- small brooms and dustpans
- static electricity research websites (See page 11 for suggestions.)

Teacher Preparation

1. Prepare the four stations prior to student participation. You may wish to do all the stations simultaneously, or spread them out over a period of days.
    Note: If running water is not available, skip Station 3.

2. Familiarize yourself with the concepts of static electricity prior to using the stations. Use the information on page 85.

3. Determine how and when pairs of students will rotate through the stations. Plan on 10–15 minutes per pair per station.

4. Print out and assemble the *Static Electricity* journal pages for each student.

5. Consider creating charts, graphs, or spreadsheets to record group responses as part of the culminating events.

6. Have materials and notebook pages accessible for the demonstrations.

Static Electricity (cont.)

Student Preparation

1. Have the materials for these experiments available for the students to explore on their own prior to this activity. Factor in time to practice blowing up balloons.

2. Explain that each student will blow up and tie a balloon to use at the first station. This balloon can be used in all four stations.

3. Post an enlarged copy of the vocabulary page and/or ask students to create illustrated vocabulary cards.

Introduce the *Static Electricity* Activities

1. Divide students into pairs to participate in four separate static electricity experiments. Each pair will conduct its own experiments using balloons and a variety of other materials including socks, water, their own hair, Styrofoam pieces, and string.

2. Discuss the procedure for each experiment with the whole group. Don't demonstrate though, as you do not want to give away the results. Review information as needed.

3. Distribute a *Static Electricity* journal to each student to be used to record his or her findings. Later, they can share the journals with their families.

4. Have each student blow up a balloon and tie the end so that the air stays in. Assist as needed, and be certain to have additional balloons on hand.

5. Have students measure the circumference of their balloons to see how large they are. Have them wrap a string around the balloon and then check the measurement on a yardstick. Or, if handy, use a measuring tape.

6. Encourage students to use the new vocabulary words while completing the experiments.

Teacher Alert: Make certain that there are no grooming or personal hair issues prior to the experiments at Station 1. Adjust activities accordingly.

Static Electricity *(cont.)*

Station 1 – Hair-Raising Feat! *– Science/Engineering/Math*

Tools

- 9" or 11" blown-up balloons—(prepared earlier by students)
- *Static Electricity* journal
- crayons, pencils
- scissors
- yardsticks
- yarn or string

Procedure

1. Measure out an 18" length of yarn or string. Compare strings with your partner to make certain lengths are the same.

2. Tie the strings to the tied ends of the balloons.

3. Rub one balloon on your hair at least 10 times. Then move the balloon near your partner's hair. Observe what happens.

4. Switch roles and repeat the experiment using your partner's balloon and hair.

5. Record observations in your *Static Electricity* journal.

Station 2 – Static Styrofoam! *– Science/Engineering/Math*

Tools

- 9" or 11" blown-up balloons (prepared earlier by students)
- large trays or cookie sheets with edges
- Styrofoam pieces to fill trays
- small brooms and dustbins
- *Static Electricity* journal
- crayons, pencils

Procedure

1. Recharge the balloon by rubbing it 10 times on your hair.

2. Pour Styrofoam pieces in the trays to fill them.

3. Move the balloon over the top of the tray of Styrofoam pieces.

4. Observe closely. What happens to the Styrofoam pieces?

5. Record your observations in your *Static Electricity* journal.

Static Electricity *(cont.)*

Station 3– Wild Water! *– Science/Engineering/Math*

Tools

- cold water source, faucet that can be adjusted to a steady stream downward.
- 9" or 11" blown-up balloons (prepared earlier by students)
- *Static Electricity* journal
- wool or acrylic socks
- crayons, pencils
- timer

Procedure

1. Turn on the faucet so there is a thin, steady stream of cold water.
2. Next, **charge** the balloon. Set the timer for 15 seconds and rub the balloon on your hair until the timer goes off.
3. Move the balloon near the stream of water. Do not let the balloon touch the water.
4. Observe closely. What happens to the stream of water as the balloon approaches?
5. Record observations in your *Static Electricity* journal.
6. Charge the balloon again. This time use a wool or acrylic sock. Does it make a difference?

Station 4– Move That Can! *– Science/Engineering/Math*

Tools

- 9" or 11" blown-up balloons (prepared earlier by students)
- empty soda cans
- *Static Electricity* journal
- crayons, pencils

Procedure

1. Lay the can on its side on a flat surface.
2. Recharge the balloon by rubbing it on your hair.
3. Hold the balloon close to the can, but don't touch the can. Did it move?
4. Record what happens to the can in your *Static Electricity* journal.

Static Electricity *(cont.)*

Culminating STEM Activities – *Science/Technology/Engineering/Math*

1. Ask each student to share one fact or discovery about his or her electricity experiments. Encourage students to share experiments they tried, and discuss what worked and what didn't. What might they try next?

2. Have students create illustrated covers for their *Static Electricity* journals.

3. At the conclusion of the experiments, send home the Family Connection letter (page 93), the student *Static Electricity* journals, and a balloon. Remind students to complete the page and return it to class. Then, provide an opportunity for students to share their families' responses to the activities. Did anything surprising happen?

4. Review and update the brainstorming chart that was created when introducing this topic with students. Have students experienced any new examples of static electricity?

5. Determine if answers to the initial questions have been discovered, or if further investigation needs to take place. Research and design further experiments if there are still unanswered questions.

6. Challenge students to conduct research online to discover additional facts about electricity and which materials are the best conductors. Then complete the following electricity experiments:

   —Experiment with various types of fabric or carpet samples to determine which materials work the best to charge a balloon.

   —Observe the reaction of holding a charged balloon near a variety of materials (felt, paper, wood, utensils, or stuffed animals) to determine which type of material is most easily repelled or attracted to the balloon.

7. Create a graph or chart and document the materials that repelled or attracted the balloon. Add pictures or create a video documenting the experiments. Try to make this an ongoing activity.

8. Have a "Can Rolling" contest. See how far cans can be rolled using the charged balloons. Measure distances with a yardstick or place a sticker on the side of the can (as a marker) and count the rolls.

Station 1 – Hair Raising Feat!

I charged the balloon on my hair. Then I moved it near my partner's hair.

This is what happened to my partner's hair.

①

Station 2 – Static Styrofoam!

I charged the balloon on my hair. Then I moved it over the Styrofoam pieces.

This is what happened to the Styrofoam pieces.

②

Station 3 – Wild Water!

I used my hair to charge the balloon. Then I moved it near the water.

This is what happened.

I used a sock to charge the balloon. Then I moved it near the water.

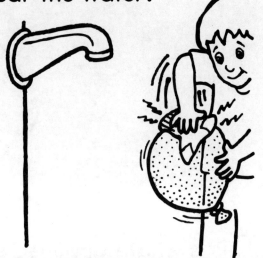

This is what happened. ③

Station 4 – Move the Can!

Draw an arrow to show what happens to the can.

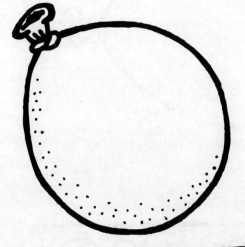

Does it roll *away* from the balloon or *to* it? ④

Student's Name: _____

Date: _____

Hello,

We have been experimenting with static electricity and your child has completed several project-based STEM static electricity experiments using balloons, his or her hair, Styrofoam pieces, and water from the faucet. Please look at his or her *Static Electricity* journal to see the results of these experiments. Then, help your child blow up the attached balloon to demonstrate some of the experiments we did.

The journal and these questions will help you to learn more about **STATIC ELECTRICITY** with your child.

- What does it mean to "charge" a balloon? What is the best method?
- What happens if the balloon is not charged?
- What does the balloon do to your hair? Why?
- Does water bend away from the balloon?
- Can a balloon pick things up?
- What other objects can you charge and use to conduct these experiments?

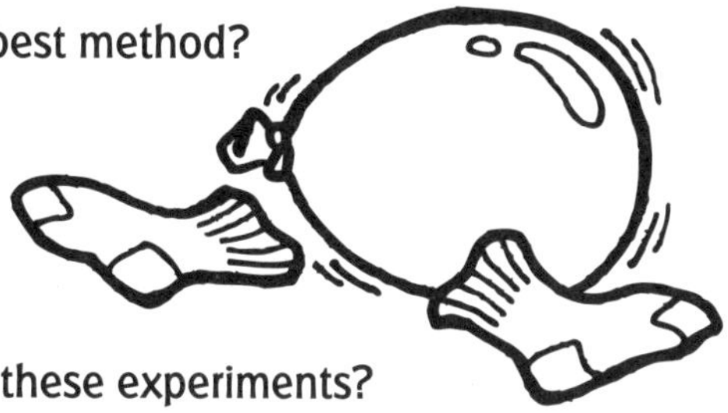

Directions: Draw a picture that illustrates one of your family member's observations while experimenting with static electricity.

Try charging a balloon and holding it over small pieces of torn up tissue paper. What happens?

_____

_____

Three-Dimensional Designs

STEM Objectives

1. Students will research and identify the types of buildings found in their community and apply that information to plan, design, and construct buildings using 3-D shapes to create a community.
2. Working in small groups, students will identify, construct, and combine 3-D shapes to form the buildings identified.
3. Data will be collected, recorded, and evaluated using charts, graphs, and/or spreadsheets.

Introduce the Topic – Three-Dimensional Shapes

1. Read a nonfiction book about 3-D shapes and about city buildings. Discuss the types of 3-D shapes that are found in buildings using appropriate vocabulary. (See page 96.)

Suggestions

3-D Shapes (My Path to Math) by Marina Cohen

A 3-D Birthday Party (Rookie Read-About Math) by Ellen B. Senisi

A Year at a Construction Site (Time Goes) by Nicholas Harris

Block City by Robert Louis Stevenson and Daniel Kirk

Building a House by Byron Barton

Cubes, Cones, Cylinders, & Spheres by Tana Hoban

Finding 3-D Shapes in New York City by Julia Wall

How a House Is Built by Gail Gibbons

Iggy Peck, Architect by Andrea Beaty and David Roberts

Living in Urban Communities (First Step Nonfiction) by Kristin Sterling

2. Discuss the meaning of *community* and the different types of buildings found in communities.
3. Introduce 3-D shapes using wooden or foam examples. If none are available, see #3 in the Teacher Preparation section on page 97.
4. Go online as a whole group using an interactive whiteboard or projector to find additional information regarding solid geometry (3-D shapes) and buildings in the community. Check the websites on page 11.
5. Share nonfiction and fiction books about 3-D shapes, cities, and communities. Discuss each book after it has been read, and keep copies on display.

Three-Dimensional Designs *(cont.)*

Brainstorming Sessions

1. Spend some time identifying 3-D shapes in the classroom. Later, extend the search to students' homes and your community. Ask:

    *   What 3-D shapes can you identify in the classroom? at home?
    *   What 3-D shapes are found in buildings? How do they fit together?
        Example: A pyramid shape might be found on top of a rectangular prism or cube shape.

2. Create a chart or spreadsheet like the one below of the 3-D shapes that the students identify. Keep adding to it.

Three-Dimensional Shapes			
cylinder	can	block	
cone	safety cone		
pyramid	roof of building		
rectangular prism	tissue box	juice box	
cube	sugar cube		
triangular prism	name plate		
sphere	basketball	hanging light	orange

3. Brainstorm and create a list of buildings that would be found in a community. Include enough buildings for each group to choose at least one for each student. For example: schools, churches, restaurants, police station, fire station, fast food restaurant, grocery stores, supermarkets, service stations, train stations, houses, apartments, hotels, parks, hospitals, specialty stores, malls, etc.

3-D Shapes Vocabulary

3-D shapes are shapes that have three dimensions—*height*, *depth*, and *width*.
2-D shapes have length and width but no depth. They are flat.

Can you find 2-D shapes in the 3-D shapes below? Trace the 2-D shapes with one color crayon. Finish tracing the 3-D shape with a different color crayon.

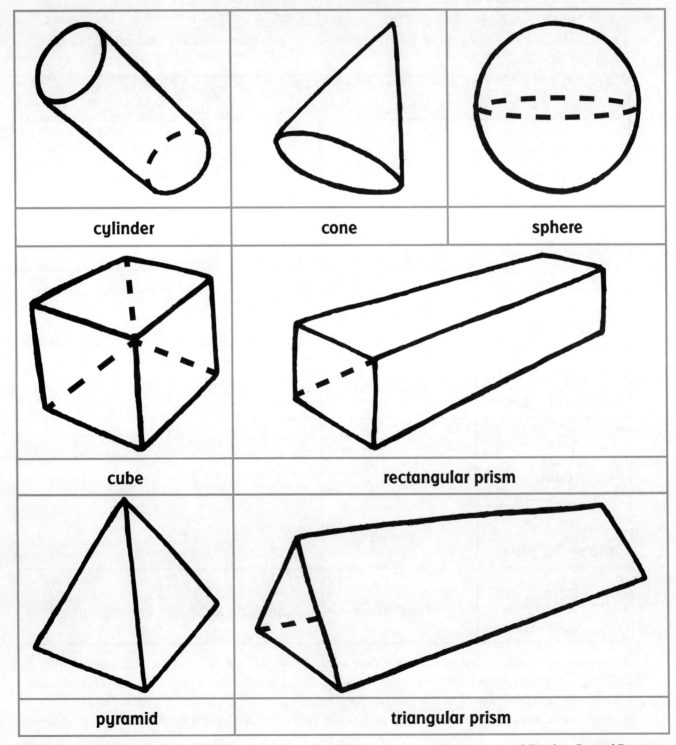

| cylinder | cone | sphere |

| cube | rectangular prism |

| pyramid | triangular prism |

Three-Dimensional Designs

The following project-based activities for 3-D designs are designed to encourage collaborative learning. Students should work in groups. Encourage students to notice when they are using *science, technology, engineering,* or *math* during their 3-D explorations.

Supplies

- items to add details to buildings—buttons, sequins, beans, pasta, rice, ribbon, yarn, string, chenille sticks, wire, labels, straws, toothpicks
- tape—masking tape and clear adhesive tape (one roll of each per group)
- 3-D shapes cardstock patterns on pages 107–112 (one set per group)
- 9" x 12" cardstock or heavy construction paper (variety of colors for each student)
- empty boxes, cardboard tubes, and containers (collected earlier)
- crayons, colored pencils, pencils, permanent markers
- digital camera
- measuring tapes, rulers, yardsticks, scissors
- poster board (one per group)
- set(s) of solid shapes (wooden or foam)
- sketch books or clipboards with drawing paper
- white glue, Tacky Glue, and glue sticks
- *3-D Designs* notebook (pages 104–106) for each student
- fiction and nonfiction books about communities and 3-D shapes (See page 94 for suggestions.)
- 3-D designs research websites (See page 11 for suggestions.)

Teacher Preparation

1. Send out the Family Connection letter (page 98) the week **before** the unit begins in order to gather the 3-D materials requested (empty boxes, cardboard tubes, etc.).

2. Print out and assemble a *3-D Designs* notebook for each student. Consider adding additional blank pages for sketching buildings.

3. Prepare cardstock patterns of 3-D shapes. Plan to assemble one set with students at the beginning of the unit. **Hint:** See if your set of foam or wooden solid shapes matches the patterns provided. If so, use the solid shapes as forms for the patterns.

4. Create charts, graphs, or spreadsheets to record group responses.

5. Plan for the *Three-Dimensional Design* project to take place over the course of at least one week. It might work best to focus on one activity or station per day for this unit. Storage space or bins will be needed for the construction items when not in use.

6. Document the project at each stage of development. Enlist students to help display the pictures and write short explanations.

Student's Name: _____

Date:_____

Hello,

Next week, we will be starting an exciting **Three-Dimensional Designs** project, which includes the study of 3-D shapes and the buildings in our community.

While working on this project your child will be focusing on the following STEM objectives:

Science – constructing 3-D shapes; experimenting to determine the best adhesive materials to use (tape, glue, etc.) to assemble the project

Technology – using computers to research 3-D shapes and different types of buildings; using digital technology (cameras) to record the project at various stages

Engineering – determining ways to construct 3-D shapes using a variety of materials; problem solving to determine how to best configure the shapes to construct buildings; planning the layout of our community

Math – identifying 3-D shapes; measuring and dividing property (mapping) for buildings

We need your help to build a community of our own based on our research and plans.

Please save empty cardboard boxes, containers, and cardboard tubes for us to use in the construction of our community.

If you have other items that might be useful for detailing our community, such as wire, small tiles, fish tank gravel, or art supplies, we would appreciate them as well.

We will have a place to store the items you donate toward our building project in the classroom, so please send them in with your student by _____.

Finally, are you a contractor, architect, city planner, or construction worker? Would you like to come in to the classroom and discuss your job and the importance of shapes in your work? We would love to have you visit. We look forward to sharing our completed community soon.

Thank you,

_____

Three-Dimensional Designs *(cont.)*

Student Preparation

1. Review the illustrated *3-D Shapes Vocabulary* on page 96. Find examples of each shape in the classroom and create a display. For example, a ball is a sphere, a can could be a cylinder, a juice box is a rectangular prism. Encourage students to be on the lookout for additional items at home.

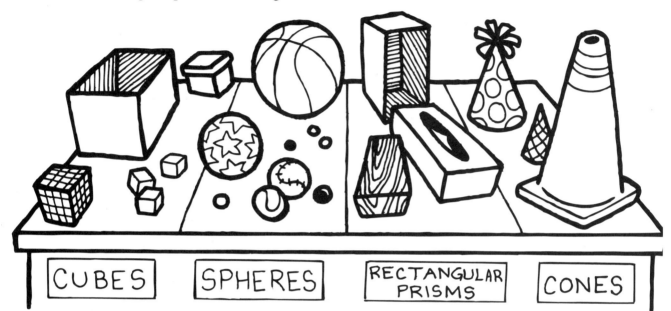

CUBES   SPHERES   RECTANGULAR PRISMS   CONES

2. Sort the empty boxes, cardboard tubes, and containers collected from home into groups to match the 3-D shapes. Create labels for each bin or pile.

3. Practice constructing 3-D shapes using the cardstock patterns or heavy construction paper and tape. How many sides does each shape have? How many bases?

4. Go on a "building walk" to find and identify 3-D shapes in buildings. Sketch the buildings to use for reference later. If possible, take photographs as well.

5. Find pictures of buildings online and post them in the classroom. Check famous ones and local ones too! Try your local Chamber of Commerce or Historical Society, or Google Earth.

Three-Dimensional Designs *(cont.)*

Introduce the *Three-Dimensional Designs* Activities

1. Divide the class into small, collaborative groups to complete the planning, designing, and constructing of buildings found in a community.

2. Give each student a *3-D Designs* notebook Explain that they will refer to the 3-D shapes in the notebook to plan and design their buildings. Provide time for students to trace and label the 3-D shapes on page 1 in the notebook. Remind them that they will need their notebooks at each station for the unit.

3. Explain that they will collaborate to build a section of a community using 3-D shapes. Mention that each group's community on the poster board base will be connected to the other bases at the conclusion of the building segment. It is important to keep the whole community's needs in mind.

4. Have each small group take turns in choosing buildings from the brainstorming list that they will build on their property. Each group member should choose a building to construct. **Each** student should record his or her group members' names and building choices on page 2 of the *3-D Designs* notebook.

   Suggestion: Try to get variety in the groups' building choices for the good of the larger community plan. One way might be to cross out a building that has been chosen. At the end, if more buildings are needed, students can discuss which buildings should be duplicated in their community.

5. Introduce the materials (poster board, tape, glue, etc.) that can be used with the collected materials to build 3-D buildings for the community. Demonstrate the activities that are to be completed before having the students break off into small groups.

6. Encourage students to use the new vocabulary words when completing the activities.

Three-Dimensional Designs (cont.)

Activity 1: Research and Design Day – *Science/Technology/Engineering/Math*

Tools

- computer access to search for images of community buildings
- crayons, colored pencils, pencils
- nonfiction books on buildings, community, and 3-D shapes
- *3-D Designs* notebooks

Procedure

1. Research online or in books to find an example of your building.

2. Draw the building in your *3-D Designs* notebook on page 3.

3. Identify the 3-D shapes in your building and list them in your notebook on page 4.

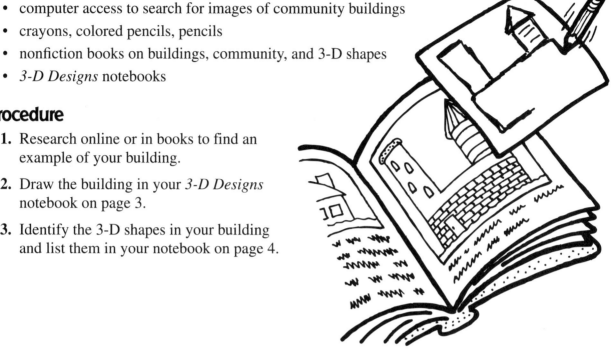

Activity 2: Community Planning Day – *Science/Engineering/Math*

Tools

- large piece of poster board (per group)
- crayons, colored pencils, pencils
- yardsticks, rulers
- *3-D Designs* notebooks

Procedure

1. Discuss how to divide the property (poster board) into sections and plan where each building will go. Determine how much space each building will need.

2. Use a yardstick and a pencil to divide the poster board into sections.

3. Label each section with the building name.

4. Color the cover of your *3-D Designs* notebook. Make any adjustments needed to the sketches.

Three-Dimensional Designs *(cont.)*

Activity 3: Construction Day – *Science/Technology/Engineering/Math*
Tools
- 3-D shapes cardstock patterns (one set per group)
- 9" x 12" cardstock or heavy construction paper (variety of colors)
- masking tape and clear adhesive tape (one roll of each per group)
- crayons, colored pencils, pencils
- empty boxes, cardboard tubes, and containers
- measuring tape, rulers, yardsticks
- permanent markers (variety of colors)
- scissors (one per student)
- white glue, Tacky Glue, and glue sticks
- *3-D Designs* notebooks

Procedure
1. Combine the found materials to construct buildings based on your sketches and plans.
2. Assemble 3-D cardstock shapes if needed for more building details.
3. Attach buildings to the marked section on the poster board.

Activity 4: Final Details Day – *Science/Engineering/Math*
Tools
- items to add details to buildings—buttons, sequins, beans, pasta, rice, ribbon, yarn, string, straws, toothpicks, chenille sticks, wire, labels, etc.
- fiction and nonfiction books about communities and 3-D shapes
- 9" x 12" cardstock or heavy construction paper (variety of colors)
- tape—masking tape and clear adhesive tape (one roll of each per group)
- empty boxes, cardboard tubes, and containers
- white glue, Tacky Glue, and glue sticks
- permanent markers (variety of colors per group)
- 3-D shapes cardstock patterns (one set per group)
- measuring tapes, rulers, yardsticks, scissors
- crayons, colored pencils, pencils
- *3-D Designs* notebooks

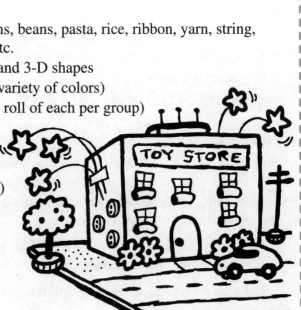

Procedure
1. Add details to buildings and surrounding area.
   - Include electric wires, cell towers, roads, etc.
   - Add landscaping including lawns, plants, trees, etc.
   - Add signs and label the buildings.
2. Draw the finished building on page 5 of the notebook, or take a picture of it and glue it to page.

Three-Dimensional Designs *(cont.)*

Culminating STEM Activities

1. Encourage the groups to collaborate and determine how to arrange each group's property to create the community.

   • Do additional roads or bridges need to be added to connect the community?

   • Are there neighborhoods? Are there any farms or gardens?

   • Is there room for a park? a bike path?

   • Is there enough parking?

   • Are there hills, mountains, lakes, rivers, or a beach in the community?

   • Are there any landmarks or statues?

2. Allow time to add more signage and details to the completed community.

3. Go on another walking tour of your neighborhood and film buildings. Have the students tally the 3-D shapes that they find along the way. Were more discoveries made? Can they spot 2-D shapes?

4. If possible, plan a field trip to a construction site to observe construction firsthand.

5. See if any parents are contractors, architects, city planners, or construction workers and could come in to the classroom and discuss their jobs and the importance of shapes in design.

6. Share the student-made community with guests. Implement additional suggestions.

7. Take photos of the completed community to add to the pictures already displayed documenting the process of creating the community.

8. Invite families and/or other classes into the classroom to view the community.

3-D Designs

Name: _____

Draw a line from the 3-D shape to its name.

cube   **cone**

sphere   **triangular prism**

pyramid   **cylinder**   **rectangular prism**

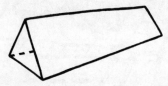 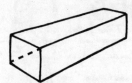

(1)

Group Members

1. _____

2. _____

3. _____

4. _____

5. _____

6. _____

Community Buildings

1. _____

2. _____

3. _____

4. _____

5. _____

6. _____

(2)

My building will be a _____.

It will look like this:

(3)

I will use the following 3-D shapes to construct my building.

I will also use these 2-D shapes.

④

My building looked like this when I was finished.

⑤

Cone Pattern

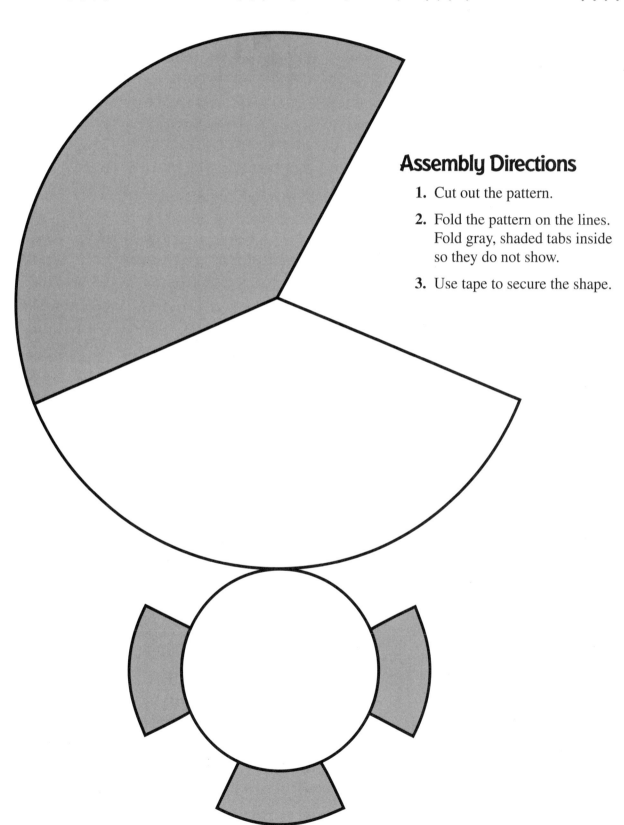

Assembly Directions

1. Cut out the pattern.

2. Fold the pattern on the lines. Fold gray, shaded tabs inside so they do not show.

3. Use tape to secure the shape.

Cube Pattern

Assembly Directions

1. Cut out the pattern.

2. Fold the pattern on the lines. Fold gray, shaded tabs inside so they do not show.

3. Use tape to secure the shape.

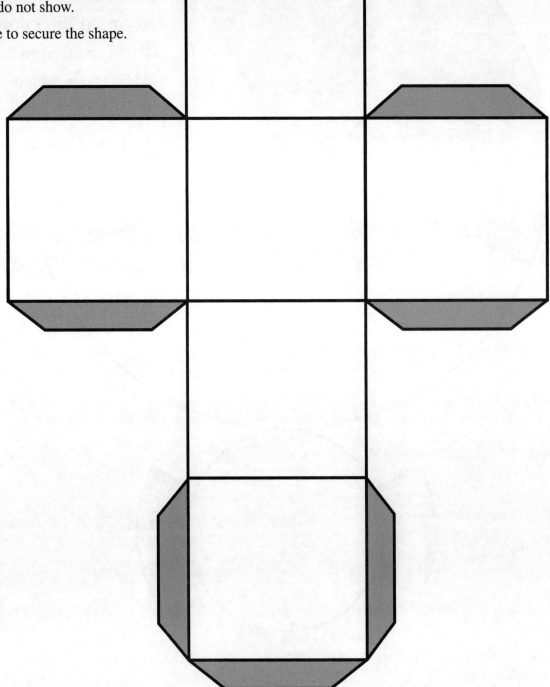

Cylinder Pattern

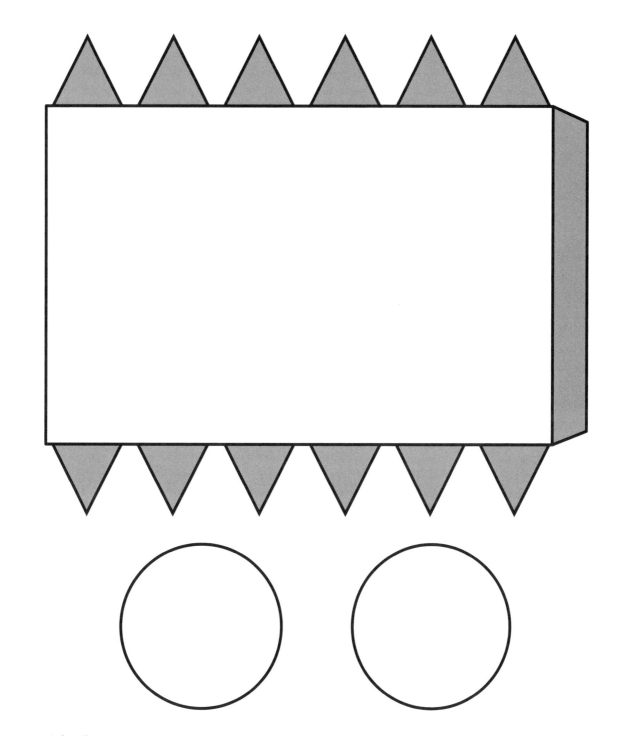

Assembly Directions

1. Cut out the pattern.

2. Fold the pattern on the lines. Fold gray, shaded tabs inside so they do not show.

3. Use tape to secure the shape.

Pyramid Pattern

Assembly Directions

1. Cut out the pattern.

2. Fold the pattern on the lines. Fold gray, shaded tabs inside so they do not show.

3. Use tape to secure the shape.

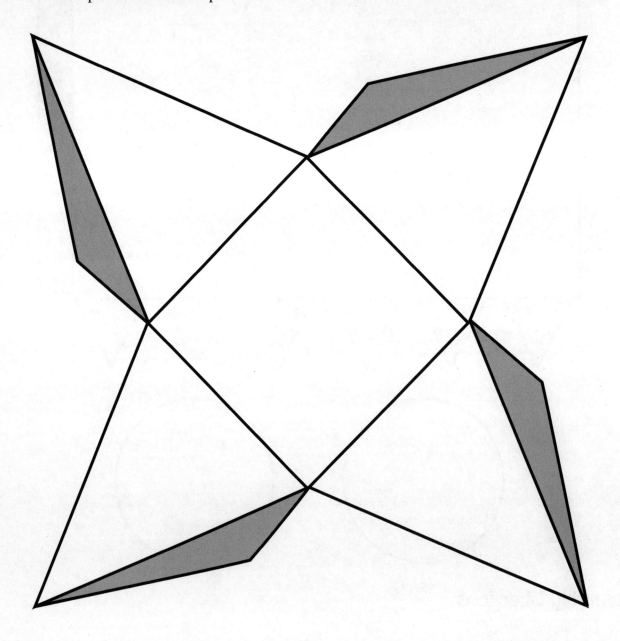

Rectangular Prism Pattern

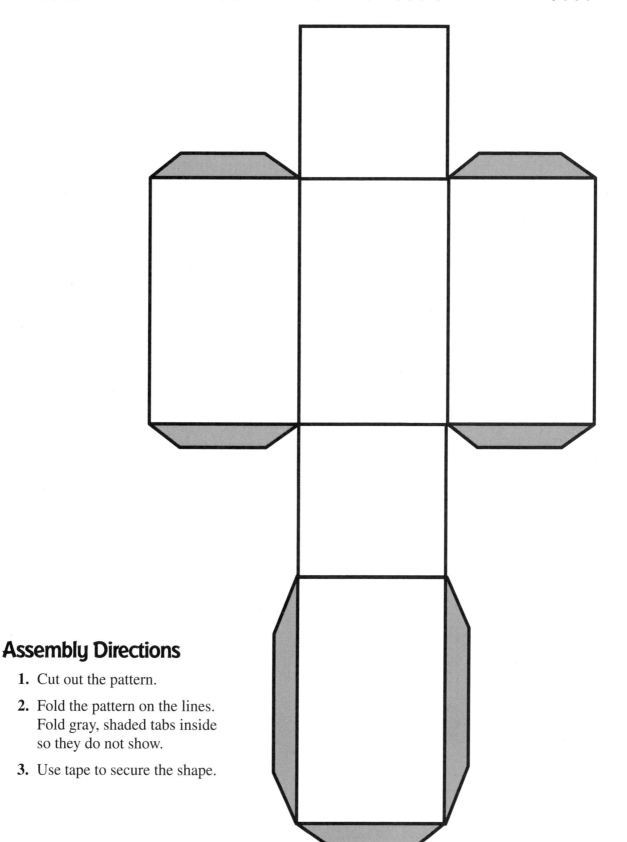

Assembly Directions

1. Cut out the pattern.

2. Fold the pattern on the lines. Fold gray, shaded tabs inside so they do not show.

3. Use tape to secure the shape.

Triangular Prism Pattern

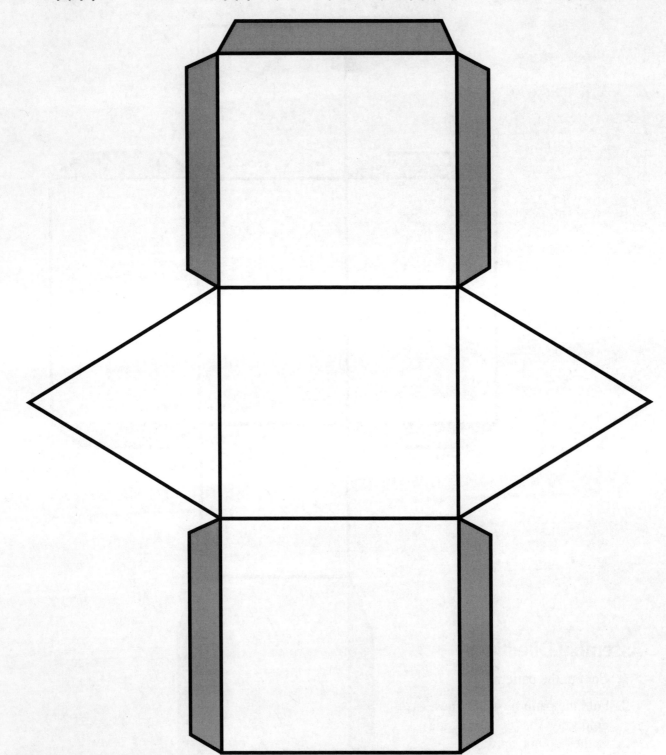

Assembly Directions

1. Cut out the pattern.
2. Fold the pattern on the lines. Fold gray, shaded tabs inside so they do not show.
3. Use tape to secure the shape.